THE
FALSE
PROPHET

BY KENNETH B. KLEIN

WPH Winterhaven Publishing House
Eugene, Oregon 97401

Scripture quotations are from the New American Standard Bible of the Holy Bible unless otherwise designated.

Cover Design
Consultant and art coordination: Fred Renich
Front cover illustration: Frank Ordaz

THE FALSE PROPHET
©1993 by Kenneth B. Klein
Published by Winterhaven Publishing House
Eugene, Oregon 97401

First Printing 1993
Second Printing 1994

Printed in the United States of America

ISBN 0-9636365-0-2

PREFACE

For over twenty years I have observed that events are fitting perfectly into the fulfillment of biblical prophecy. For those that walk closely with God these are exciting and fearful times because in them we see the signs indicating the return of Jesus Christ. Yet sadly, many have slipped away because of those very signs, and suffered the shipwreck of their faith.

God has not given up on His straying children. Let me illustrate in a true story His heart towards those who have temporarily slipped away.

On a trip to the Middle East years ago, my wife experienced a terrible accident, yet something which pictures beautifully the unchanging love of God toward us.

We were on our way from Jerusalem to Petra in Jordan, famous because it is a city literally carved into the rose-red cliffs and caves of the surrounding mountains. We stopped just over the border, in Jordan, to use the rest rooms. Sanitation in the third world is very primitive. The rest rooms were in fact open space without any private enclosures. People literally had to relieve themselves on the floor. This was especially hard on the women. Excrement was on the ground and foul smells were coming up from everywhere.

One of the women thought she had found a good spot and signaled my wife to come over by her. As she moved toward the place, the cement broke under her feet. She fell into a cesspool, up to her knees in filthy human excrement.

After my wife, three months pregnant, fell into the cesspool, the other woman pulled her out. One woman in the group had, for some reason, brought a change of clothes to the rest area. Others had jugs of water they had purchased in Jerusalem. They washed her and surrounded her to give her privacy. Then they helped her remove the defiled clothing and put on a new clean garment. So it is with God. He reaches into the filthy pit, pulls us out and hides us in His people to be cleansed and changed.

Nonetheless, this incident haunted us for a long time with fears for our unborn child. We thought about diseases and how they are communicated through human waste; cholera, hepatitis, dysentery. Only through daily prayer were we delivered from that terror as we waited the six months until the child was born. Then we found that God had protected him.

The experience had left its mark on me, however. Through it I realized what a critical period is our time of embryonic development in the womb. If we do not form properly in the womb it is a lifetime of disfigurement.

This fact led me to see that our life in this world is a time of development for eternity. Though we have nine months of development in the womb, which shapes us for this life, we have a lifetime in this world to be formed for eternal life with God.

While it is true that many times in our walk with God we stumble into problems as my wife did at the cesspool, there is another reality of which we tend to lose sight. There is a powerful evil which blinds us to the dangers we face daily. In his letter to the Galatians, Paul speaks concerning this evil power.

Grace to you and peace from God the Father, and our Lord Jesus Christ, who gave Himself for our sins, that

He might deliver us out of this present evil age, according to the will of our God and Father.

Galatians 1:3, 4

Over the years I have been troubled as I saw people fall away from Christ, no longer seeking Him or desiring to seek Him. They have come under the power of the evil one and fallen back into the filth of this life.

In biblical Greek there are two words for evil. One is "kakos", the other is "poneros". Kakos evil is benign, like an ugly wart. Poneros evil is malignant, like a cancerous growth, an evil that if not arrested will consume the whole organism. The word Paul uses for the age in which we live is "poneros", malignant.

What many today fail to understand is that the dynamic evil which has been present in the world from the beginning has been on track across time organizing itself into a unified system--a One-World Governmental System--a network of nation states under the dominion of God's arch rival, Lucifer. This system will not suddenly become apparent just before Christ returns, but is nearing completion today. There are warnings in Scripture about this system, primarily in the book of Revelation.

The cry of the psalmist to God, however, epitomizes the effect of this system on all generations:

O God, why hast Thou rejected us forever? Why does Thine anger smoke against the sheep of Thy pasture? Remember Thy congregation, which Thou hast purchased of old, which Thou hast redeemed to be the tribe of Thine inheritance; and Mount Zion, where Thou hast dwelt. Turn Thy footsteps toward the perpetual ruins, the enemy has damaged everything within the sanctuary. Thine adversaries have roared in the midst of Thy meeting place; They have set up their own standards for signs. It seems as if one had lifted up his axe in a forest of trees. And now all its carved work they smash with hatchet and hammers. They have burned Thy sanctuary to the ground; they have defiled the dwelling place of Thy name. They said in their heart, "Let us completely subdue them." They have burned all the meeting places of God in the land. We do not see our signs; there is no longer any prophet; nor is there any among us who knows how long. . . . .Why dost Thou withdraw Thy hand, even Thy right hand? From within Thy bosom, destroy them! Yet God is my king from of old, who works deeds of deliverance in the midst of the earth. Thou didst divide the sea by Thy strength; Thou didst break the heads of the sea-monsters in the waters. Thou didst crush the heads of Leviathan; Thou didst give him as food for the creatures of the wilderness. Thou didst break open springs and torrents; Thou didst dry up ever-flowing streams. Thine is the day, Thine is the night; Thou hast prepared the light and the sun. Thou hast established all the boundaries of the earth; Thou has made summer and winter. Remember this, O Lord, that the enemy has reviled; and a foolish people has spurned Thy name. Do not deliver the soul of Thy turtledove to the wild beast; do not forget the life of Thine afflicted forever. Consider the covenant; for the dark places of the land are full of the habitations of violence. Let not the oppressed return dishonored; let the afflicted and needy praise Thy name. Do arise, O God, and plead Thine own cause; remember how the foolish man reproaches Thee all day long. Do not forget the voice of Thine adversaries, the uproar of those who rise against Thee, which ascends continually.

Psalm 74

Today, the sanctuary of God's presence is the human heart. We must heed, therefore, the warning concerning the power of the poneros evil in its pervasive, unrelenting attack on the temple if we expect the image of Christ to be formed in us. When God's people fall into the world system they can no longer see, and as a result the people of the world have no prophetic voice. The church is the prophetic voice of God. How does the church get out of the cesspool? We must first admit we are in it.

The televangelists of the recent past who fell from grace hurt thousands of people because they succumbed to the love of the world. Many followed their lead and have become mired in the system that the prophets of old warned against. Therefore, what lies ahead is a 1990's birds eye view of their warnings, and brings fresh insight into a generally overlooked topic.

This book is essentially an exposition and interpretation of Revelation Chapter 13. Although it deals with the two great Beasts, its principle aim is to discover the second Beast, or the False Prophet, as he is called in Scripture. This second Beast is the one whose activity in the world unifies the rebellion against God in this realm.

The importance of this section of Scripture is that it allows for a re-clarification of a Christian world view. It is vital that the believer hold onto a Christian world view since the active evil in the world continually surrounds him. Because the values and ideals of the world are powerful forces, the believer must exercise spiritual warfare. This requires that believers have great care in living out their lives in the world.

Called out of the world to be prepared for eternity, the Christian who gives himself again to what the world has to offer becomes like the dog in the proverb who returns to his vomit, or like the sow, to wallowing in the mire.

The time has come to renew our vision of this world from God's vantage point. It is time to arise and come up to higher ground. The obstacles are great. Yet, to respond to the challenge of presenting a clear Christian world view is the purpose of this book. Hopefully these insights will help us loosen our grip on the world. Jesus is coming. Let us prepare to meet the King with the oil of the Holy Spirit in our lamps, wrapped in the robes of His righteousness.

Dedicated to
all those who love HIS appearing

Contents

Preface   5

Introduction 11

Chapters

1   The Last Stroke 15

2   The Brothers..19

3   The Mark of Cain 27

4   Heavenly Rebellion 31

5   The Unseen World 35

6   The Man of Sin 41

7   The Mother of All Harlots 45

8   Tracking the Beast 49

9   Mystery Babylon 57

10 Five Fallen Kings 61

11 Rome: The Sixth Empire 71

12 The Seventh Head 73

13 The Innate Drive 85

14 World Wars I and II 87

15 The Great Sword 91

16 The Satanic Resurrection 95

17 The Agent of antichrist 99

18 The False Prophet: The Second Beast 103

19 History of the False Prophet - The New Zion 113

20 History of the False Prophet - The Post Civil War Era ..125

21 History of the False Prophet - Anglo Americanism 133

22 The Two Horned Beast 139

23 Daniel's Seventy Weeks 147

24 Fire From Heaven 151

25 The Image of the Beast 155

26 Television - Snow White's Poisoned Apple 161

27 The Law...165

28 Here is Wisdom 169

29 Laser Scanning Systems for Supermarket Automation ..179

30 The King of the World 189

31 How Then Shall We Live 197

32 Summary 203

Chapter Notes 205

Bibliography

Index

INTRODUCTION

What was Bill Clinton doing at the Bilderberger's meeting in Baden Baden, Germany in August of 1991? Why would the Governor of li'l ole Arkansas be in attendance with such a global elite? Some of the top names that made the list, such as David Rockefeller and Henry Kissinger, everyone might expect, but Bill Clinton--way back in August of 1991? (The Spotlight, Aug. 1991.)

The Bilderberger group has been described as a secret organization very much like the C.F.R. and the Tri-lateral Commission. They are dedicated to building a New World Order. The Bilderbergers meet twice a year at some obscure but posh resort around the world. Their secret conferences are attended by leading Internationalists in finance, academics, government, business, and labor from Western Europe and the United States.

Why all the secrecy? Why are all these guys sneaking around having meetings, and after the meetings are over the world undergoes dramatic change?

In Clinton's acceptance speech at the Democratic convention in 1992 he praised the work of Dr. Carroll Quigley, who was more than any other man responsible for shaping his thinking in international affairs and economics. Who was this man?

Dr. Quigley was a professor of history at the Foreign Service School of Georgetown University. He also taught at Princeton and Harvard. Basically, it can be said that Dr. Carroll Quigley was the mentor of many of the sons of the Eastern Establishment. His most important work was *Tragedy and Hope*.

Dr. Quigley's epic volume, *Tragedy and Hope*, was a deliberate exposure of one of the best kept secrets in the world. As one of the elite insiders he knew the scope and power of the hidden government and the agenda of it's leaders in their quest to gain total global control. In his book he makes it clear time and again that he warmly supports their goals and purposes. But if that is the case, why would he (himself an insider) want to expose this world-wide conspiracy and disclose many of it's secret operations?

In his book, *Tragedy and Hope*, he says, in effect, that it is now too late for the little people to turn back the tide. His book, in effect, is an urging not to fight back. Those who do will only choke themselves to death against the noose that is being tightened around their necks. On the other hand, those who go along with the program of the elite world planners will all find themselves in a man made millennium of peace and prosperity.

Dr. Quigley, the mentor of Bill Clinton, assures us that we can trust these benevolent, well meaning men who are secretly operating behind the scenes. THEY are the hope of the world, and all who resist them represent tragedy, hence, *Tragedy and Hope*.

In the pages ahead the significance of these startling events and insights will run headlong into the fulfillment of biblical prophecy and a clear understanding of what the future holds for us all. It will soon become very evident how with great power and worldly wisdom, the manipulation of the political and economic machinery of the world has been, and is being, orchestrated by none other than the False Prophet of Revelation 13.

We need not fear, for God has not been taken by surprise at the secret workings of men, as though they have operated without His notice. As a matter of fact, he knew of these things two thousand years ago when he related them to a simple fisherman named John, who became a mighty apostle.

What men have done in the dark, God now openly declares so that you might know the nearness of the coming of Christ.

Chapter One

THE LAST STROKE

They slipped out of New York without being seen. They changed their names and rode the lowly subways. They falsified their itinerary, and in the middle of the night they made their way to the secret assignation.

Their rendezvous had been carefully prepared. Already the hideaway was sealed off and guarded in strictest isolation. All English speaking servants were released. Every possible leak of information was sealed. There was no chance for knowledge of the event taking place to slip out. What was at hand was the final episode in the conquest of the United States of America, the event that would consummate a 200 year plot to seize the hidden conduits of international capital.

This last stroke, the final blow, would effect the realization of an ancient conspiracy that would finance a new Global

World Empire. The means would be the centralization and control of mammon.

The secret location for the meeting was a millionaire's retreat off the coast of Georgia called Jekyll Island. [1] No name could have been more fitting for such a place of treachery.

The name Jekyll was immortalized by the great American author Robert Lewis Stevenson in his famous book, Dr. Jekyll and Mr. Hyde. Stevenson's masterpiece tells the story of a benevolent Dr. Jekyll, who in his laboratory discovers a drug that turns him into a beast (Mr. Hyde).

Jekyll Island, a place of seclusion and tranquility, owned by the rich and powerful, became a laboratory for concocting an evil scheme, the potion of which, once consumed by the American Republic, transformed it into a Mr. Hyde, a beast. [2] This is the true story of six thousand years of watching and waiting for the final rebellion characterized by the emergence of a Global World Government of promised peace and prosperity.

The last two centuries have seen the final chiseling on an ancient historic monument erected by the corporate will of mankind. There is an inscription at the foot of the edifice revealing a fantastic testimonial placed there by their creator: Man without God is a beast.

The Chosen Ones

For hundreds of years the people of God have been anticipating a Global World Empire ruled by the Antichrist. In the 1930s and 1940s many thought that Adolf Hitler and Benito Mussolini were the Antichrist and the False Prophet. Bible believers viewed the National Socialist German Worker's (Nazi) Party as the Beast that would fulfill the prophecy of Daniel and Revelation. In the 1960s scholars and spokesmen from Dallas Theological Seminary, and books such as Hal Lindsay's *The Late Great Planet Earth*, focused the North American church, both Protestant and Roman Catholic, on the European continent as the place where the Beast would rise with his ten horns or kings. [3]

When it became known that the European Common Market would be limited to ten nations, it seemed clear to many that those nations comprised the ten kings. It looked as though the European nations perfectly fit into the fulfillment of Daniel's and John's prophecies.

A horn in Scripture is interpreted as a king or a kingdom, so the announcement created much interest and excitement in the church world. However, the ten nations have now grown to twelve, and the excitement has waned.

Many are perplexed and confused trying to figure out how it all fits together. Although the Common Market has expanded to twelve nations, along with Eastern European nations as well, there will be principally ten nations out of them all that give their allegiance and power to the Antichrist and comprise the power locus just as Daniel and John predicted. And the Global World Empire will be located in the area of the old Roman Empire.

But how has this come about? Who and what are moving the world toward this One-World Empire? What role did these powerful men who gathered at Jekyll Island play in the formation of a Global Empire?

The Instruments of Satan

From the time of man's departure from God in the Garden, history has recorded the efforts of the god of this world (Satan) and his relentless movements to bring about the consolidation and control of this planet. The idea that a man can be righteous in himself without a spiritual rebirth is the tune, played on the flute of the Pied Piper of Hell, which has for some 6000 years made the children of Adam dance to his song.

Though powerful spiritual forces have been at work behind the scenes, man has over the millennia dutifully and collectively worked on the Earth to bring about the final rebellion against God in this neo-Babylon called the New World Order. Some men have taken actual oaths to the devil himself, and knowingly set themselves to battle against God. Others have unwittingly become ensnared in the plot to overthrow God's place of Lordship. In this war there is no middle ground, one is either for or against the Lord. The battle lines have been drawn in the spiritual realm, and very soon the Mark of the Beast will draw the final battle line on the earth. Whoever is on Satan's side of that line has no hope.

From Nimrod to Caesar, from Weishaupt to Hitler to the Antichrist himself, the events of history have been, and are being, orchestrated towards a One-World Government and the worship of a man—a man who will one day sit on top of it all proclaiming himself to be king of the world—Satan's prince, the Antichrist.   Through technological advancements, religion, politics, and money, the world has been seized and is being moved ever closer to that day.

Now, even as the cornerstone of the Global World Order is being laid, the people of the world are unaware of the terrible trap that is about to snap closed upon them. Where are the sons of light? Where are the prophets—the Daniels, the Jonahs, the Jeremiahs? Who will declare this age? Can't anyone see?

Chapter Two

THE BROTHERS

Unless a kernel of wheat falleth to the ground and dies it abideth alone; but if it dies it bringeth forth much fruit.

John 12:23 KJV

So begins one of the greatest Russian novels of all time, *The Brothers Karamazof* by Dostoevsky. Dostoevsky was concerned about man's conscience and his responsibility for his brother. This theme ripples through the book. The question, "Am I my brother's keeper?" is not addressed anywhere better than in the book of Genesis.

At the dawn of history, Adam and Eve, the progenitors of the entire human race, gave birth to two sons and named them Cain and Abel. The lives of these brothers are symbolic of two great spiritual truths. A careful analysis will reveal the two truths and explain the forces which have worked through time shaping the whole of human history.

Cain was a tiller of the soil and Abel was a shepherd of sheep. When the time came to worship God (Genesis 4:3, 4), Cain offered the fruit of the ground. Abel took one of the first born of the flock in his charge and slew it before the Lord. According to the Scripture, Abel's offering was accepted by God while Cain's was rejected.

The question naturally arises, why did God accept the offering of Abel and reject that of Cain? A close inspection of each brother's appeal to God will reveal the role of the two principles of life which emanate from them and flow like rivers through the course of human history and that govern the conscience of every human being that was ever born. In Abel we have the Mystery of Righteousness, and in Cain the Mystery of Iniquity.

The Two Trees

The Mystery of Righteousness corresponds to the tree of life, which Scripture mentions in the Garden of Eden. The Mystery of Righteousness was the life of God and was the tree from which man was allowed to partake freely when he lived in the original state God had intended.

The life of God is eternal life. As long as man ate of that tree he could live forever. But God had also placed in the garden another tree. This was the tree of the knowledge of good and evil. God commanded man not to partake of this tree. The tree created a dilemma for man. Through this dilemma, God established man as a sovereign entity by giving him the opportunity to exercise choice. He could choose either to continue to partake of the tree of eternal life, or he could partake of the tree of the knowledge of good and evil.

There was another consideration attached to the exercising of choice: God said regarding the tree of the knowledge of good and evil, "in the day that you eat from it, you shall surely die," (Genesis 2:17). There was a dire consequence for disobeying God's directive. Notice that the tree gave knowledge of both good and evil, not just evil. Just what in actuality was this tree? The tree of the knowledge of good and evil represented the Law.

In the Mosaic Law the commandment, "Thou shalt not steal" established the fact that stealing is contrary to God's righteous nature. On the other hand, it implied that the reverse is true, not stealing is righteous or good. Here is a demonstration of the knowledge of good and evil as defined by the Law that separates good and evil.

Eating the fruit in disobedience to God had terrible consequences. Not only did breaking God's Law mean death, it meant that one was all the more bound by the Law. The rule of law simply served to show how far short man falls from measuring up to God's standard. The Law itself does not enable or empower men to act righteously. The very life of God in the tree of life produced the righteousness which the tree of the knowledge of good and evil could not. The tree of the knowledge of good and evil was a curse in that it gave a knowledge of righteousness because it could divide between good and evil, but it could not produce righteousness.

The partaking of the tree of the knowledge of good and evil produced the fruit of death. The deadly fruit reaped by Adam and Eve has overtaken the entire human race. All of humanity is their offspring—all are born under the Law, under the curse of the tree of the knowledge of good and evil.

The Mystery of Righteousness
The Tree of Life

When Abel took a lamb and sacrificed it to God, his act of worship demonstrated a recognition and fundamental understanding of the human predicament. Abel saw himself defiled and separated from a holy God with no means of restoration. In humility Abel came before God, acknowledging his need for a clear and clean conscience. He knew that if he was to gain freedom and release from past transgressions, it was up to God.

Abel's recognition of his own depravity allowed him to position himself before God with a recognition of his transgressions and their affect on his conscience. Though the Law did not come until Moses, Abel knew the truth because the Law was written on his heart. He recognized that his fallen nature was prone to continually miss the mark of God's standard of perfect righteousness. No matter how sincere and consistent his efforts to conform to righteousness, he was trapped in his fallen nature—a slave of his inability to live the Law.

Abel's sacrifice to God was not a representation of his own labor. On the contrary, it was a representation of his recognition that by no work of his own could he ever gain the approval and acceptance of God in a restored relationship with Him. Abel's sacrifice was accepted by God because it was an offering based upon his need, not his effort. He appealed to God on the basis of God's mercy, not his own deserving.

In Abel's sacrifice we have the prototype and embodiment of the Messianic mission of Jesus, who is, Himself, the sacrificial Lamb. Christ fulfilled the requirements of the Law. He was the perfect sacrifice which Abel's sacrifice foreshadowed and foretold.

Cainism

The knowledge of iniquity comes from a knowledge of the Law, for the Law explains good and evil. The greater the knowledge, the more profound the effect upon the conscience because of greater awareness of the morality of behavior. This was Cain's irreconcilable predicament. Cain's offering to God in worship was essentially a representation of the work of his hands. Cain sought approval and relationship with God on the basis of his human effort and labor. He was the embodiment of the self-made man.

Cain is the antithesis of Abel. Cain's perception of himself became the focus of his sacrifice for atonement. His attempt at relationship with God was not acceptable because it was not based upon a recognition of his need (Genesis 4:5-7).

In his approach to God each brother's thought-life was totally and forever set. Abel's approach brought acceptance and peace. Cain's approach brought rejection; and anger, hatred, and murder filled his heart.

From conscience emerges thought, which produces behavior. Thus conscience, whether based upon proper or improper relationship with God affects thought-life, and, subsequently behavior. This principle of action as the outworking of conscience applies to individuals singularly or to corporate bodies, as the collective conscience of a group (or even of a nation or state). An example of this on a group level would be the vigilantism of a mob lynching. The mob, trying to right a perceived wrong, collectively commits the sin of Cain (i.e. murder).

Grasping the critical lesson of the story of Cain calls for great objectivity through which the impact of these principles on the whole of human history may be observed. Failure to grasp the importance of the story may result in vulnerability to deception by the spiritual forces that operate behind the scenes— forces that have weakened the Christian world view.

Cainism has weakened the Christian world view in our time. What is Cainism? It is man's approach to God on the basis of his own good effort. It can best be illustrated by pointing out some of its most obvious manifestations in our own culture. In America we have recently seen great displays of a cultural/state civil religion, evidenced in "We Are the World", "Hands Across America", and also in the great spectacle of the refurbishing of the Statue of Liberty. Even the Gulf War revealed the elements of civic state religion. These events portray human effort as being able to set the world straight—the instrument that can right the ills of the world and bring in peace and safety.

The effects of Cainism can also be seen in contemporary religion with its focus on self-esteem. In true Christian faith, Scripture instructs man to lose himself by focusing on loving God and neighbor, as opposed to the modern philosophies of self discovery. Yet, the pervasive power and self-righteous appeal of Cainism is causing great deception. Many are unwittingly being set up for Cainism's crowning achievement, the Antichrist.

Are we being too hard on our culture? Not if the cultural/state religious ethic is more prominent than the biblical ethic. The cultural ethic amounts to an approach to God that represents the finest work of man. This will happen on a grand scale when nations conspire to finally establish a New World Order, and bring a temporary peace. It will be a rerun of Cain's offering. No matter how good the works, even of the magnitude of a New World Order, mankind is still left with a stained conscience. This isn't to say that doing good is wrong, but rather, we must accept the fact that doing good isn't good enough to gain the approval and acceptance of God.

When the spirit of nationalism (the synthesis of the spirit and will of the members of the nation state) rises higher than the Spirit that glorifies Jesus Christ, the state has become deified, and we have fallen into idolatry.

Cain was egocentric in that he thought he could better himself, and his position with God, on the basis of his own effort. He failed to recognize his inherent evil nature and God's solution for his situation. In his confusion Cain sought to establish his own righteousness by human endeavor.

Abel's sacrifice, on the other hand, was not aimed at impressing God with how good he was, but rather was an honest recognition of the hopeless predicament he was in, so he cast himself on God's mercy. Thus Abel's offering foreshadows Messiah's death on the cross as man's only means of salvation and recovery from his predicament (Hebrews 11:4). Herein lie the two principles that dichotomize the undercurrents of all human thought and behavior—and all human history. Since man cannot live with his guilty conscience, he must select either Cain's approach to God or Abel's.

On the surface Cainism looks more powerful, has more appeal, and also seems more righteous. This is because it caters to the ego of man, and gives expression to man's need for purpose and meaning in life. This type of fulfillment is a temporal avenue and does not take into account man as a son of God, or his need for an *eternal* answer and meaning for existence.

The collective guilt of the nations, arising as a result of ignoring Abel's sacrifice, provides an open door for the emulation of Satan's lust for power and a reenactment of his pursuit of it, and is the driving force of the enormous effort toward the construction of a New World Order.

Abel's sacrifice, by prefiguring the cross of Christ, laid the basis for a clear conscience before God, and therefore the ability to partake of the life of God, which is peace.

All of history has been shaped by the two principles embodied in the lives of these two brothers. Cainism, with its refusal to concede the inherent brokenness of man's nature, strives vigorously, but futilely, for a self-adjusted conscience through good works. Abelism represents the basis of the New Covenant, which rests on the foundation that "without shedding of blood there is no forgiveness," (Hebrews 9:22)

The world views of the brothers are in direct collision, and their corresponding self-concepts are in direct opposition. They are totally irreconcilable and can never merge. The divergent philosophies that have been built on these two spiritual roots have affected the nature and expression of every human being and nation state that has ever existed.

Chapter Three

THE MARK OF CAIN

> A nd the Lord set a mark upon Cain lest
> any finding him should kill him.
> Genesis 4:15

The Mark of Cain has been a point of discussion and debate since time began. Since the time when all of Cain's descendants died in the biblical flood, however, there is no longer a literal mark. What has remained is the symbolic significance of the mark and its new emergence characterized in the Mark of the Beast.

The mark that was placed upon Cain by God was the result of Cain's murder of his brother. Actually, it represented Cain's failure by allowing sin to have mastery over him. Cain was envious and hateful towards Abel, who found favor with

God, and so Cain slew him. These two men, both literally and symbolically, represent the two principles that operate the human conscience.

Abel's relationship with God is evidenced in the sacrificial system of the Jews, and in the sacraments, born again experience, and transformed life of the believer within the church. It's final form will be the millennial reign of Christ.

Cain's system can be seen as the Gentile world governmental systems and *all* religion where *law* is exalted. It's final form will be the Global World Government of the Antichrist, which is called the Beast system. The Beast and all whose names are not written in the Book of Life will be marked with the neo-mark of Cain, called the Mark of the Beast.

Neo-Cainism

The Mark of the Beast, as it is mentioned in Revelation 13, is the representation of the highest technological-cultural-economic system and religious worship incorporated into an identification mark. The mark represents the highest corporate achievement of the human race, and is the crowning work of mankind; the utopia that all have dreamed about since time began, and man's attempt to return to the Garden of Eden.

The mark identifies all who receive it as those who believe in the finest, most positive, most altruistic qualities of the human being. It is a system that will exalt man and point to him as the center of the universe. In other words, it encompasses everything that man is and all he has done collectively from the beginning until now towards his effort to establish world peace and safety in FORTRESS EARTH.

This colossal effort is the last days offering of Cain once again. And once again it will be rejected by God. But all those that buy into the system knowingly or ignorantly will receive on their hand or forehead the neo-mark of Cain, the Mark of the Beast.

What is the Mark of the Beast?

In the pre-Christian era there was one who was given great insights into these mysteries. His name was Daniel.

Daniel's writings unfold the beginning of insights into the mysterious Mark of the Beast.

God presented the Gentile world governments to the Hebrew Daniel as though they were beasts, wild animals that ignore the reign of God over them (Daniel 7:1-12). He saw the ruling Babylonians as a roaring lion, while the coming Medo-Persian empire he viewed as a bear. The Greeks he saw as a leopard with two wings, and the last ruling empire was different than all the rest. The last empire was explained as a beast which had no earthly counterpart; it had ten horns, and then one little horn.

The apostle John caught a vision of this system some six hundred years after Daniel. In Revelation 13, this last great world gentile power was actually completed by another Beast that had two horns (Revelation 13:1-11). This second Beast, which has been much wondered and talked about for the past two thousand years, uses principally three different abilities or tools to finish constructing the Beast System (Revelation 13:13-18)

1.   Fire that comes down from heaven
2.   An image that speaks and has spirit life
3.   A mark, which is 666, and without which no one will be able to buy or sell

The last of these three abilities is called the Mark of the Beast.

The Mark of the Beast is the most talked about feature of the abilities of the two-horned Beast. The mark obviously relates to some kind of economic system that will do away with the necessity for gold or currency. It is an economic system which is different than anything that has appeared in history. It is a system that all must participate in or else go without buying or selling. In other words, a cashless society.

Chapter Four

HEAVENLY REBELLION

According to several Old Testament passages (see Ezekiel 28, Isaiah 14, and Genesis 1), prior to the creation of man, God set up His government in the spiritual realm with governing principalities. Three of the most powerful of these entities were archangels. Their names were Michael, Gabriel, and Lucifer.

Many people today regard this history as mere myth. Especially in the western hemisphere and the industrialized nations, very little credence is given to the existence of a spiritual realm. In these nations utilitarianism and materialism tend to pervade the consciousness of the average citizen. For many the spiritual realm seems to have little relevance to their daily needs.

Nevertheless, Scripture records that God did create spiritual beings to govern His kingdom. The most powerful and talented of all was Lucifer. The prophet Ezekiel was given great understanding into Lucifer's beauty, authority and power (Ezekiel 28:13-19).

Lucifer was God's chief assistant, and had a vast network of subordinates that assisted him in the work of governing with which he was charged. We would do well to consider this powerful position Lucifer had in God's government.

He was the angel that covered, or was established to guard. His great beauty and splendor were unparalleled, his musical talent unmatched in all the universe. He was the master of commerce and trade.

Although God in His foreknowledge recognized the troubles the future held, He entrusted Lucifer with great knowledge, insight, wisdom and understanding into the workings of God's kingdom.

Lucifer's pride in himself was insatiable. When it caused him to seek the very throne of God, to attempt to usurp and overthrow God's rule, he was cast out of his position and imprisoned on a speck of dust called Earth. What a judgement! His freedom and authority had spanned the infinite heavens, and now he was a convict imprisoned on a tiny planet somewhere in space.

God's anger would not rest with this judgement alone. The disloyalty of Lucifer created a tremendous void in the government of God. Scripture records that one third of all the created beings in God's government were cast out with him. Lucifer was able to carry off with his rebellion one third of the angelic host (Revelation 12:4).

The enormity of this loss, though on a lesser scale, would be like losing the U.S. Congress and still trying to run the government of the United States. The government literally would be unable to function properly.

The Lord wasn't taken by surprise, however. He had already predetermined a plan of recovery and restoration. He created man to take Lucifer's lost position. This added to Lucifer's judgement as he would have to witness his replacement being raised up before him.

When man was created he was assailed by Lucifer and deceived and enticed into following him. Lucifer on Earth is known as Satan. Since the beginning of human history Satan has been working to gain total control over the Earth by setting up a government that he would rule and in which he would be worshipped. The same wickedness he demonstrated when he originally sought God's throne, he is exhibiting on the Earth.

God in His majesty and foreknowledge intercepted Satan's attempt to destroy mankind by sending Jesus to rescue the human race. With his government gaining momentum Satan, the deceiver, would have us believe that Christ's rescue mission failed. There are even religious cults that claim this to be so, but it is far from the truth.

In the face of Satan's New World Order, Jesus Christ is calling out a special people to follow him. These elect people, whom He calls His saints, are being raised up to be transformed into the image of Jesus Christ as they live out their lives awaiting the appearance of their King. Discerning the contrast between God's kingdom and Satan's is part of the process of being transformed and following Jesus.

Further, as the saints are being developed to fulfill their eternal destiny with Christ they will face conflict and resistance from the forces allied with Satan's movement toward a One-World Order. This is to be expected. The saints are required to resist the devil, and stand for righteousness. They are instructed to pray, "Thy kingdom come, Thy will be done, on Earth as it is in heaven." (Matthew 6:10). They are required to "fight the good fight", (1 Timothy 6:12) and to "not love the world" (1 John 2:15).

Without God's viewpoint and perspective on the world, the subjective predicament and pressure from environmental factors becomes so overwhelming that it becomes exceedingly difficult to stand strong in faith. God wants His saints to understand the enemy's plan so they will resist his deception and maintain the vigilance of faith.

What lies ahead is Satan's program for the New World Order.

Chapter Five

THE UNSEEN WORLD

Throughout Scripture, there are passages alluding to the spiritual realm which was formed by God before the material realm was created. Two of the most notable passages on this subject are in Isaiah 14 and Ezekiel 28.

> How you have fallen from heaven, O star of the morning, son of the dawn! You have been cut down to the earth, you who have *weakened the nations*! But you said in your heart, I will ascend to heaven; I will raise my throne above the stars of God, I will sit on the mount of assembly in the recesses of the north. I will ascend above the heights of the clouds; I will make myself like the Most High.
>
> Isaiah 14:12-14
> (emphasis mine)

Again the word of the Lord came to me saying, "Son
of man, take up a lamentation over the king of Tyre,
and say to him, 'Thus says the Lord God, "You had
the seal of perfection, full of wisdom and perfect in
beauty. You were in Eden, the garden of God; every
precious stone was your covering: the ruby, the
topaz, and the diamond; the beryl, the onyx, and the
jasper; the lapis lazuli, the turquoise, and the emerald;
and the gold, the workmanship of your settings and
sockets, was in you. On the day that you were
created they were prepared. You were the anointed
cherub who covers, and I placed you there. You were
on the holy mountain of God; you walked in the
midst of the stones of fire. You were blameless in
your ways from the day you were created, until
unrighteousness was found in you. *By the abundance
of your trade you were internally filled with violence, and
you sinned*; therefore I have cast you as profane from
the mountain of God. And I have destroyed you, O
covering cherub, from the midst of the stones of fire.
Your heart was lifted up because of your beauty; you
corrupted your wisdom by reason of your splendor.
I cast you to the ground; I put you before kings, that
they may see you. By the multitude of your iniquities,
in the unrighteousness of your trade, you profaned
your sanctuaries. Therefore I have brought fire from
the midst of you; it has consumed you, and I have
turned you to ashes on the earth in the eyes of all who
see you. All who know you among the peoples are
appalled at you; you have become terrified, and you
will be no more."'"

Ezekiel 28:11-19
(emphasis mine)

Since the fall of Lucifer there has been a powerful
negative force operating in this unseen spiritual realm which
has victimized man in ways he simply cannot perceive. The
world has been brilliantly organized by Satan into a complex
system of politics, economics, philosophy, education, culture,
science, and religion.

Religious Deception

Although Satan operates in every area of deception, he is especially adept at religious confusion. As stated above, he was in the Mountain of God. The term Mountain of God refers in Scripture to the government of God.

> But the stone that struck the statue became a great mountain, and filled the whole earth.
>
> Daniel 2:35

Lucifer's great understanding of the things of the Lord made it easy for him to arrange counterfeits of God worship. The eastern religions, for example are masterpieces of religious confusion designed to deceive the multitudes. Space does not allow for a discussion of the religions, including some Christian groups, that have careened off the pathway of truth.

Since the discovery of Satan as the serpent in the garden, there has always been an executive power on earth for the completion of his goals. The end of it all will be a global kingdom for the Devil himself. The world will see the results of his incredible, brilliant power in his ability to finalize his plan to bring almost total obedience and worship to himself through a One-World Government.

This process of many millennia is speedily reaching its final form, in all probability before the end of this present century. That there is a definite strategy at work to bring this about is stated and restated throughout the Old and New Testaments. The strategy is clearly evidenced throughout ancient history, and is displayed in the atrocities of Adolf Hitler's Third Reich in this present century.

Unfolding Satan's Plan

It is not the intention here to speculate on the future, but to lay out historic and current trends that are in alignment with the ancient prophetic writings. Therefore, what is being set forth is not intentionally predictive, but rather interpretive, that we might clearly see the hour in which we live and how we should live in this hour.

Let us consider how to stimulate one another to love
and good deeds, not forsaking our own assembling
together, as is the habit of some, but encouraging one
another; and all the more, as you *SEE THE DAY*
drawing near.

Hebrews 10:24-25
(emphasis mine)

The Day of Christ is rapidly approaching. We must stay
attuned to the signs. Scripture predicts that there will be "wars
and rumors of wars" (Matthew 24:6) Nation will rise up against
nation; famines, pestilence, and earthquakes are all part of the
last days scenario that will overtake the inhabitants of Earth. It
is as though the earth is groaning, like a woman about to give
birth. As we get closer to the end these pangs will get closer and
be of greater duration.

Signs of the Times

As one travels to a city, signs along the way tell how far
away it is. Scripture indicates that there will be specific signs to
watch for, indicating the nearness of the Day of the Lord. The
most important of these signs is mentioned in 2 Thessalonians
2:1-3.

Let no one in any way deceive you, for it will not
come unless the apostasy comes first, and the man of
lawlessness is revealed.

2 Thessalonians 2:3

There have been those who tried to force this passage by
using the Greek text to say the word *apostacia* actually means a
departure from the earth. The word departure, they say, is
actually a reference to the Rapture. (This is the great translation
of the saints mentioned in 1 Thessalonians 4:16, 17).

The laws of interpretation, hermeneutics, call for the
weight of Scripture, meaning what does the rest of Scripture say
about this topic? The weight of Scripture decidedly leans
toward an interpretation of the word *apostacia* as a departure
from *the faith.*

The Great Falling Away

But the Spirit explicitly says that in later times some
will fall away from the faith, paying attention to
deceitful spirits and doctrines of demons.

1 Timothy 4:1

The Lord Jesus himself said in Matthew 24 that many
would depart from the faith. This word apostacia used in 2
Thessalonians 2 does not indicate a rapture reference.

The context indicates that before the Day of the Lord
there will be a time of *darkness* such as the world has never
known. It is the powers of darkness that cause many people to
abandon their faith in Christ. In the final onslaught by the
powers of the evil one many will be lost.

The loss of the restraining force in the great falling away
enables the Antichrist to appear and set up his world kingdom.

Chapter Six

THE MAN OF SIN

The Man of Sin will be manifest before the Day of Christ. The importance of this sign is noted by Scripture, and it is the second clearest sign of the advancing Day of the Lord.

> That you may not be quickly shaken from your composure or be disturbed either by a spirit or a message or a letter, as if from us, to the effect that the Day of the Lord has come. *Let no one in any way deceive you, for it will not come unless the apostasy comes first, and the man of lawlessness is revealed, the son of destruction.*
>
> 2 Thessalonians 2:2-3
> (emphasis mine)

The church should be looking for the coming of Jesus by paying attention to the advancing of the Antichrist and his system called the Beast. The Antichrist will be the commander-in-chief of the notorious Beast system that was foretold in the books of Daniel and Revelation.

The signs of the Day of the Lord were carefully pointed out to those who lived in Thessalonika. The Thessalonians were instructed to keep their eyes not only on the clouds, but on the earth as well. Jesus said,

> But when these things begin to take place, straighten up and lift up your heads, because your redemption is drawing near.
>
> Luke 21:28

Where to Look

When the prophet spoke, in Daniel 9:26, of the people of the prince to come as the ones that would destroy the temple of God in Jerusalem (which occurred in 70 A.D.) inadvertently he was giving us a clue as to where and who the Antichrist would be.

He will be a western man, and the location of his great kingdom will be in the area that comprised the old Roman Empire. That is because it was the Romans under Titus who almost 2000 years ago began to set the stage for the coming world dictator. The Romans were the people of the prince to come that Daniel was referring to.

The present day location of the old Roman Empire is Europe. Through the unification of the Common Market by various treaties and economic ties, the stage is now set for the advent of the Antichrist.

How He Will Approach

By taking a look at the past we can see the unfolding of prophetic events. The spiritual cataclysmic event of Lucifer's mutiny and his resulting judgement, as presented in Isaiah 14, Ezekiel 28, and Revelation 12 bring out two key thoughts:

1.   Satan was cast down to weaken the nations. The weakening of the nations, as Ezekiel pointed out, was effectualized by the abundance of trade, or merchandising.

2. His celestial beauty and spiritual knowledge he corrupted and uses to deceive the world.

Beauty, or appearances, and money, or mammon, the equivalents of power and spiritual knowledge, are the instruments through which he brings confusion over all the earth.

Manifestations of His Agenda

The spiritual effect of Satan's control of the world can be most easily seen in the multitude of religions worldwide. But his agenda also includes a One-World Government, with a man of his choosing at the head of it.

Satan has been working for thousands of years to set up his earthly throne. As we approach two thousand years since the birth of Christ we are very near the completion of Satan's world government. Let us trace the progression of his efforts.

Chapter Seven

THE MOTHER
OF ALL HARLOTS

An understanding of Mystery Babylon is foundational to understanding Satan's work in the world from Eden to the present.

In the book of Revelation, perhaps the most celebrated language that symbolizes the worldwide religious confusion engendered by Satan is seen in the great harlot of the 18th chapter. We find her referred to in highly symbolic language, *Mystery Babylon the Mother of Harlots.* Many have offered interpretations of this mystery woman, but by and large she is a false representation of God's true church on the earth, who goes about seducing the inhabitants of the earth through false doctrines and perverted ideas of God (Revelation 18:1).

In both Revelation 17 and 18 that there seem to be two facets to Mystery Babylon. Mystery Babylon Mother of Harlots, and

Mystery Babylon the Great City. It is clear that a distinction must be made between the two.

Mystery Babylon Mother of Harlots is clearly a global religious order that operates under Satan to deceive the whole world religiously. Mystery Babylon the City is a commercial-industrial complex that operates in conjunction with this pseudo-religious matrix. This satanically backed mystical industrial complex is the foundation of the prophesied Beast System of both the prophet Daniel and the apostle John.

The Birth of the Beast

After the world was destroyed by the biblical flood, it was repopulated by Shem, Ham, and Japheth and their descendents. Nimrod, a descendant of Ham began the organization of great cities, building the first great city in the post flood era (Genesis 11:1-9).

> Now Cush became the father of Nimrod; he became a mighty one on the earth. He was a mighty hunter before the Lord: therefore it is said, "Like Nimrod a mighty hunter before the Lord."
> Genesis 10:8, 9

The expression that he was a mighty hunter before the Lord can carry a hostile meaning—the word *before* being sometimes used as meaning against the Lord. The Jewish encyclopedia says that Nimrod was he who made all the people rebellious against the Lord. [1] During his time, Nimrod fit the picture of the Anti-christ, who was predicted later. One day, according to God's word to Eve, there would come a deliverer. God said:

> And I will put enmity between you and the woman, and between your seed and her seed; He shall bruise you on the head, and you shall bruise Him on the heel.
> Genesis 3:15

Many believed Nimrod was the promised Messiah, and looked to him as the savior of the world. There were many reasons why the people felt this way.

He was a mighty hunter. When ferocious animals roamed in great numbers, people lived in constant dread for their lives. Nimrod hunted down and killed these animals and tried to make life safer for the people.

He even conceived of greater ways to defend and protect the people. He invented the concept of walled cities, the first of which was the city of Babylon. It is easy to see why he was greatly admired and revered by the peoples of the world and looked upon as the promised one. [2]

Nimrod organized Babylon into a great worldwide commercial center and then went into surrounding areas establishing his control and prominence. He later developed a religious system that was based upon the arrangement of the stars, which today is known as the zodiac, and from which comes the idea of astrology. Babylon, which in Hebrew means the gate of God, also comes from a similar Hebrew root word balal, which means confusion. [3]

Mystery Babylon the Mother of Harlots and Babylon the City, the commercial center are both mentioned in the book of Revelation as the end-time promulgators of Satan's program for world control, and are located and found here in ancient Nimrodian Babylon. [4]

Nimrod, an Antichrist

It can be seen that Nimrod the humanitarian, and the one heralded as a savior of the world, was a classical Antichrist. He led the people away from worshipping the living God into idolatry. He taught the worship of life through mystery religions and worship of the stars. He taught the worship of the creation, and left the creator out of the picture. [5]

The power of Nimrod's control over the known world in many ways can still be felt today. For example: The tradition of the keeping of the Christmas tree during the season of the celebration of Jesus' birth is actually a stolen idea from the celebration of the birth of Nimrod. The Roman Catholic church adopted the idea, which was a world renowned pagan tradition, and applied it to the birth of the Lord Jesus. [6]

From the beginning Satan's executive power has been behind the world political/economic and religious empires, begin-

ning with Babylon. It will end with a Global World Government
for the Devil himself.

Chapter Eight

TRACKING THE BEAST

The Scripture below, expressed in symbolic form, lays down the panorama of Gentile world-rule and power from the time of the Egyptians until the final world gentile empire is formed.

> And the angel said to me, "Why do you wonder? I shall tell you the mystery of the woman and the beast that carries her, which has the seven heads and the ten horns. The beast that you saw was and is not, and is about to come up out of the abyss and to go to destruction. And those who dwell on the earth will wonder, whose name has not been written in the book of life from the foundation of the world, when they see

the beast, that he was and is not and will come. Here
is the mind which has wisdom.

The seven heads are seven mountains on which the
woman sits, and they are seven kings; *five have fallen,
one is,* and the other has not yet come; and when he
comes, he must remain a little while. And the beast
which was and is not, is himself also an eighth, and is
one of the seven, and he goes to destruction. And the
ten horns which you saw are ten kings, who have not
yet received a kingdom, but they receive authority as
kings with the beast for one hour. These have one
purpose and they give their power and authority to
the beast."

Revelation 17:7-13
(emphasis mine)

The Seven Heads

This Scripture pictures a relationship between Mystery
Babylon, who is called the Great Harlot, and the infamous beast
upon which she is seated. Her seated position suggests that she
is in control and being carried by the Beast. Although much
biblical scholarship has been put forth concerning the heads of
the Beast as being literal mountains or literal hills (i.e. that the
seven hills of Rome were the mountains upon which the Harlot
sat; the Great Harlot being Rome), Scripture goes on to point out
that the seven mountains are seven kings. The angel says they are
seven regal mountains, seven kings, seven great ruling powers.

A mountain, or prominent elevation on the surface of the
earth is one of the common Scriptural images, or representations
of a kingdom, regal dominion, empire, or established authority.
So King David, speaking of the vicissitudes which he experienced as the king of Israel says, "O Lord, by Thy favor Thou didst
make my *mountain* to stand strong." (Psalm 30:7).

The Lord in His threat against the throne and power of
Babylon said:

"Behold, I am against you, O destroying *mountain,*
who destroy the whole earth," declares the Lord,
"And I will stretch out my hand against you, and will

roll you down from the crags, and I will make you a burnt out *mountain."*

Jeremiah 51:25

But the stone that struck the statue became a great *mountain,* and filled the whole earth.

Daniel 2:35

The seven heads are best explained as seven kings. The symbolism of the mountains or heads merely represent seven successive kingdoms. It can be argued that although heads may be kings or kingdoms, why should it be said that they are successive? The fact that five of the heads had already fallen, one was then in existence, and one was still future answers that objection.

Since the issue of succession of kings is evidenced in the above Scriptures the identity of Mystery Babylon Mother of Harlots cannot be Papal Rome. The woman sits upon empires that had already fallen and continues to outlive the empires that come and go. She rides upon empires, kings, powers of the world; inspires, leads, and controls them. She is above them all, so that they court her, are bewitched and governed by her--governed not with the reins of empire, but with the lure of her fornication. Mystery Babylon is none other than Nimrod's Babylon that continues to hold sway, outliving each successive empire.

Her doom is at the end of time, when she receives her judgement, and therefore fills up the whole interval of time since the foundation of the Babylon of Nimrod.

The Ten Horns

The last great empire of the gentile rulers will consist of a ten-member confederacy that incorporates essentially the same territory controlled by the Romans during the time of Christ.

The ten members of the Beast are spoken of as horns. A horn in Scripture is interpreted as a king or a kingdom. Daniel said:

Then I desired to know the exact meaning of the fourth beast...and the meaning of the ten horns that were on

its head.... 'As for the ten horns, out of this kingdom
ten kings will arise.'

Daniel 7:19, 20, 24

These ten kings or kingdoms give their power and authority
to the Antichrist for one hour, or a short time.

The seven heads represented in the vision are seven world
gentile powers, or imperial heads, that have existed during the
history of the world. They will be the focus of investigation over
the next few chapters. Remember that the goal of this process of
investigation will be the revelation of the identities of both the
first and second Beasts of Revelation chapter 13. It is imperative
that we study both Beasts, for it is through the identification of the
first Beast that the necessary clues emerge to identify the second.

Ten Horns and Seven Heads

Each head in the symbol represents an imperial Empire.
These imperial heads along with the ten horns (and the little horn
of Daniel 8) comprise the entire Beast that was, and is not, and is
about to come. It can be seen immediately from this Scripture that
the Beast will not be just a last days phenomenon, but has been
Satan's executive agent in some form for over 5000 years.

The last phase of the Beast system will evolve to a climax
where ten kings or kingdoms will give their allegiance to a man
(the Antichrist) who will operate the Global World Empire. This
evolutionary process began after the foundation of Babylon the
Mother of Harlots and has proceeded through each empire to the
present (Revelation 13:1).

The construction of the Beast system corresponds with the
words of Christ when he spoke of the times of the Gentiles. "And
Jerusalem will be trampled underfoot by the Gentiles until the
times of the Gentiles be fulfilled" (Luke 21:24). The times of the
Gentiles simply means the period of time when the world is run
by empires controlled by the Gentiles.

Many believe the times of the Gentiles ended when the state
of Israel was formed in 1948, and when Jerusalem was recaptured
by the Jews in 1967. But the end of the Beast system will come,
and the destruction thereof, when Christ returns to establish His
Kingdom on the earth for one thousand years.

You continued looking until a stone was cut out
without hands, and it struck the statue on its feet of
iron and clay, and crushed them. .... But the stone that
struck the statue became a great mountain and filled
the whole earth.

Daniel 2:34, 35

This Scripture points to the coming Kingdom of God, which
strikes the existing governing powers and topples them. It is a
kingdom cut out without hands, which signifies a kingdom not
man made. It will come at the end of the world, and it alone will
destroy the kingdoms (the Beast) of the Gentiles (Daniel 2:44, 45).

The Spiritual Template

Cainism and Mystery Babylon are, and always have been,
the principle guiding powers of each subsequent and succeeding
imperial head from its rise to its fall. These guiding powers will
come to their zenith in the Antichrist's Global World Order.
Revelation 17:10, 11 provides a historical template to show each
imperial head from the time of its beginning until the present.

The Beast--The System

And they are seven kings; five have fallen, one is, the
other has not yet come; and when he comes, he must
remain a little while. And the beast which was and is
not, is himself also an eighth, and is one of the seven.

Revelation 17:10, 11

John saw the Beast as a system, whereas Daniel saw both the
Antichrist and the last stage of the Beast system (the ten horns).
When John spoke of the eighth head, he was speaking of a
revived world imperial system that had recovered from a head
wound, or as the Scripture put it, the wound of a *great* sword.

And I saw one of his heads as if it had been slain, and
his fatal wound was healed. And the whole world was
amazed and followed after the beast.

Revelation 13:3

Today there are some who think that the apostle was talking about a man that had been healed from a wound to the head. They believe that this alleged human being would then turn into the Antichrist, a satanic resurrection as it were, but Scripture speaks of an imperial head being resurrected, not a human being.

Unlocking the Mystery

To get at the mystery of who and what the eighth head is, we must see who the seventh head is, since it preceeds the eighth head (the eighth head is of the seven). Getting to the root of this mystery takes some digging because we must reconstruct the whole system in its entirety.

> And they are seven kings; five have fallen, one is.
> Revelation 17:10.

We will begin here with the term *one is*. What does this mean? This was clearly the world empire that existed during the time Jesus walked the earth, and also the time when the apostle John was writing the great book of Revelation. It was the Roman Empire.

Moving backward from the Roman Empire, signified by the head that is, the sixth head, there had been up to that time five world empires that had fallen, which were of the same class as Rome. A brief look at history tells us with unmistakable certainty who these five empires are.

The Five That Had Fallen

In retreating sequence the five fallen empires are:

1. Greece
2. Medo-Persia
3. Babylon (under Nebuchadnezzar)
4. Assyria
5. Egypt [1]

These are the five kings that had fallen. Rome was the sixth, the one that is. The task ahead is to identify the empire that is called the seventh, from which comes the eighth. First we will briefly walk through the five fallen kings looking for clues to the identity of the last two empires.

Chapter Nine

MYSTERY BABYLON

C ritical in understanding the five fallen kings is how the
ancient Babylonian kingdom of Nimrod relates to
the empires that would follow it. Babylon, the mysterious
system, is represented in the book of Revelation as a scarlet
woman, or a prostitute, and is entitled Babylon the Great, the
Mother of Harlots and of the Abominations of the earth (Revelation 17:5).

In Egypt, according to Hislop, the worship of the patron god
and goddess, Osiris and Isis, can be directly traced to Nimrod,
founder of the great Babylon, and his wife Semiramus. [1]

As a man of renown upon the earth, Nimrod advanced his
kingdom from Babylon into Egypt, then into Assyria, and then to
other parts of the world. His greatness as a mighty hunter, and

the protection he afforded the masses by fortifying the cities with walls, caused great admiration by the peoples of the earth.

It was through fortification that the peoples enjoyed peace and safety from the ever present threat of wild beasts. Nimrod became legendary amongst the peoples of the earth for these mighty exploits. [2]

Hislop records that in his hunting expeditions Nimrod employed the horse, along with leopards to track down animals. His renown became universal, and Nimrod was deified by man and hailed in the eyes of the peoples as a savior. The ancient Babylonian coins that picture a centaur (half horse and half man) is the actual depiction and memorializing of Nimrod. [3]

Yet for all the good he did for the people in saving and protecting them from destruction, Nimrod turned the heart of the peoples from God unto himself. [4]

Desecrated Trinity

In ancient times, the recognition of the Trinity was universal in all the nations of the world, but in the pagan world it was overlaid with idolatry. Nevertheless, even the corruption of the idea of the Trinity proved how deep seated this idea was in the breast of man. Pagan religion was replete with symbols that attested to this idea of a triune God. [5]

It was, however, during the Babylonian era, that an important change occurred in the pagan concept of the Trinity. The God triune was clearly articulated in the Christian era, but during Nimrod's time there consisted a blasphemous idea of the Father, Seed or Son and Holy Ghost. It came to have been thought of as the eternal Father spirit of God incarnate in a *human mother*, and a divine son. As a result of this alteration in the original idea of the triune God, the first person of the Trinity, the Father, was now overlooked. Now with the change, the Babylonians focused their worship on a goddess mother, and a son. [6]

Since Nimrod had expanded the sphere of his influence and power into Egypt, these people also began to worship the mother and the son under the names of Isis and Osiris. Isis the mother, and Osiris the son. [7]

As Nimrod's fame spread, the Babylonian godhead became a universal focus of worship. In India the gods Isi and Iswara are the counterparts of the Egyptian Osiris and Isis, and are worshipped even to this day. In Asia the same holds true with Cybele and Deous as the facsimile of the Egyptian duo, and in pagan Rome it was Jupiter-puer. In Greece, the godhead was Ceres, the great mother with the babe at her breast, or Irene, the goddess of peace with the boy Plutus in her arms. Even in remote places, such as, Tibet, China, and Japan, evidences were found of this same pagan worship of a misunderstood idea of the Trinity. [8]

Hislop makes tremendous application of this perversion of the Godhead and its effect on papal Rome, where Mary and Jesus have become the Christian counterparts of Egyptian Isis (the mother) and Osiris (the son). [9]

The Wife of Nimrod

The depth of this mystery is great, with many turns in the road. In order to be able to arrive at some clarity of thought concerning the issue, we must go to the origin and centerpiece of the mystery, Nimrod and his wife Semiramus.

Semiramus, who had been known as the wife of Nimrod, evolved as time passed to a lofty position as mother of Nimrod as well. In Egypt, Isis was the mother and wife of Osiris, but these were merely Egyptian names attributed to the great fortress builder Nimrod and his wife/mother Semiramus. In Egypt Osiris bore the title, "husband of the mother". [10]

One last point needs to be hammered home before we press on to the next fallen king. In the ancient book of the prophet Daniel (Daniel 11:38) we read of a god called Ala-mahozine, the *god of fortification*. Since Antichrist honors a god of fortification, it is important to identify what and who this god was.

> But instead he will honor a god of fortresses, a god
> whom his fathers did not know; he will honor him
> with gold, silver, costly stones, and treasures.
> Daniel 11:38

Although nowhere in antiquity can a god of fortification be found, there is great evidence of a goddess of fortification. Her name is Cybel, and she is always seen with her crown turreted, as are the fortifications of towers. The reason for the towers of her crown was due to the fact that she erected towers in the cities she ruled over. [11]

The first city erected after the ancient world was destroyed by the great flood was Babylon. Ovid, the great historian, tells us that it was Nimrod's wife Semiramus, the first Queen of that city, who was believed to have surrounded the city with brick. Semiramus, the deified queen, became the prototype of the goddess of fortifications. Cybel, with her turreted crown, was also known as Rhea, and Semiramus was know as Rhea at times as well. Cybel was actually another name for Semiramus. [12]

But Semiramus (Rhea) did not build the walls alone. It has been kept as a matter of record by the Bible (also through the ancient historian Megasthenes), that it was Nimrod who surrounded the Babylonian city with the wall. Yet, Semiramus gained the glory because she came in the esteem of the ancient idolators to hold a higher position than Nimrod, and attributed to her were all the characteristics and successes belonging to her husband. She was, however, the counterpart of the deity (Nimrod deified) presiding over the bulwarks or fortress. From this we can see that the god of fortresses is none other than Nimrod. His deified name in Babylon was Ninus (meaning, the son). [13]

Egypt, Free Masonry, and the New World Order

It is an admitted fact that the secret system of Free Masonry was originally founded on the mystery religion of the Egyptian Isis, the goddess mother/wife of Osiris. In Isis, the Egyptian counterpart for Semiramus, Nimrod's deified wife/mother, we have a very important connection with Mystery Babylon of the Masonic lodges of the church era in the Western world, both Europe and the United States of America.

What could have united the Masonic body with the mysteries if the mysteries had not had particular reference to architecture and building, and had the god of the mysteries not been celebrated for perfecting the arts of fortification and building?

These mysteries of Free Masonry learned from Egyptian mythology, and indirectly from Babylon, would be applied to Fortress earth; the obvious relationship of Free Masonry to empire building, and global planning for a New World Order.

Chapter Ten

FIVE FALLEN KINGS

The First Fallen King - Egypt

The Egyptian civilization arose after Nimrod's ancient Babylon, and is believed to be over 5,000 years old. The Egyptian people were a very spiritual people, and firmly believed in an after-life. They held to the Babylonian notion of a pantheon of gods, and their spiritual history is well documented. The most important archeological discoveries of their religious history can be found in the Valley of the Kings. There in Luxor, Egypt, on the walls of the caves of the entombed pharaohs, are the hieroglyphic codes that have maintained the record. [1]

The character of the images kept on the walls of the caves suggests a very curious sense of how the Egyptians perceived the spiritual world. The deities pictured have animal heads and human bodies. Such a strange synthesis suggests a real, or imagined quality of the animal, and made identification of the deity easy.

The temple of Karnak was the country's largest, and was dedicated to the god Amon-Re, the sun god. The most important gods, however, were Osiris and his wife Isis. Osiris ruled over vegetation and the dead. Isis represented the devoted mother and wife. Their son was Horus, the god of the sky. [2]

When kings ruled ancient Egypt, the Egyptians believed that each of the pharaohs was Horus in human form. This legend greatly strengthened the authority of the kings. Strengthened by this myth, their authority had tremendous impact on every aspect of the people's daily life. [3]

Although the earliest beginning of Egyptian society dates back some 5,000 years, it wasn't until 1554-1304 B.C. that Egypt became the world's strongest power. Much of the prominence and power of the nation was a result of the large and permanent army, and the advanced military techniques they had learned from earlier periods. The Egyptians also developed a galley powered navy with which they made many military conquests into Southeast Asia. [4]

This great world empire, the first of the five heads of the Beast mentioned in Revelation, reached its height around 1400 B.C. under King Thutmose III when he brought Palestine and Syria under Egyptian control.

The infamous Rameses II, the oppressor of the Hebrews, reigned during Egypt's 500 years of world dominance known as Dynasty XIX. It was during his reign, however, that the great Egyptian empire began to decline. [5]

The Second Fallen King - Assyria

Clearly the influence of Nimrod was established in Assyria, as Scripture points out in the book of Genesis. The principle city of Assyria even bears the name of Nimrod (in that Ninus, his name deified, is the principle root of the city's name, Nineveh). [6]

The Assyrian king was known as the great king, the legitimate king, the king of the whole world. In the Assyrian kingdom the figure of a bull represented the king. The same word that signified bull, signified also a ruler or a prince. The horned bull signified the *mighty prince*, which was a direct throwback to Nimrod, and represented all the great Assyrian kings. [7]

Although the Assyrian civilization can be traced back to 2,000 B.C., its empire building actually took place around 800-606 B.C. The story of Assyria is in the main a story of the Assyrian kings. Some of the greater kings were Shalmaneser, Tiglath-pileser, and Esarharden. These kings, along with others, led a proud, cruel and warlike race.

In many respects they were much like Rome, for just as Rome welded all the peoples of the Mediterranean world into a great empire, then throughout her domain scattered seeds of her civilization, so did Assyria weld into a great empire the numerous petty, warring states and tribes of Western Asia. Afterwards, throughout her extended domains she spread her civilization, which to a great degree she had received from conquered Babylon. [8]

As the empires that succeeded her evolved and came to the forefront, it is not an exaggeration to say that the great civilization of Greece owes much of her architecture, her sculpture, her science, her philosophy, and her mathematical knowledge to the Assyrian empire.

Assyria was a mighty power for hundreds of years, but after the mid 600s B.C., she declined as a world empire. Babylon was coming to the forefront as a world power. [9]

The mighty influence of the Nimrodian Babylon (Mother of Harlots) can be clearly seen in the Assyrian empire.

The Third Fallen King - Babylon

Babylon had two runs as a world empire: Nimrod's Babylon, which was recorded in Genesis chapter 10, and dates back to 5000 B.C., and Babylon, which arose to supplant the Great Assyrian Empire during the 600s B.C., reaching its peak from about 625-538 B.C. [10]

The question might be asked at this point, why was not Nimrod's Babylon of old considered as the first of the five fallen kings mentioned in Revelation 18?

A good, but improper, answer would be that if you started with Nimrod's Babylon you then would proceed forward to

Egypt, then Assyria, Babylon again, Medo-Persia, and Greece. This would equal six fallen kings and would be too many to fit into prophecy.

It could then be argued, however, that beginning with Egypt and finishing with Greece is forcing the Scripture to say what you want it to say. Nimrod's Babylon should be the beginning point.

This point of view is not an unfair argument, but when the whole of Revelation 17 is looked at it becomes clear why this is not so.

> And one of the seven angels who had the seven bowls came and spoke with me, saying, "Come here, I shall show you the judgement of the great harlot who sits on many waters, with whom the kings of the earth committed acts of immorality. . . . ."
> And he carried me away in the Spirit into a wilderness; and I saw a woman sitting on a scarlet beast, full of blasphemous names, having seven heads and ten horns. And the woman was clothed in purple and scarlet, and adorned with gold and precious stones and pearls, having in her hand a gold cup full of abominations and of the unclean things of her immorality, and upon her forehead was written, a mystery, "BABYLON THE GREAT, THE MOTHER OF HARLOTS AND OF THE ABOMINATIONS OF THE EARTH."
>
> Revelation 17:1-5

From this Scripture it can be seen that Nimrod's Babylon is the fountain head, or the progenitor of the global world kingdoms, and sits atop them as a ruling power. It is the ruling posture of the woman (Nimrod's Babylon) that elevates her importance above the succeeding fallen kings, beginning with Egypt, and ending with Greece, thus eliminating her as one of the fallen kings. Each successive king, as we continue on, emanates from her and continues to have intercourse with her.

Modern Babylon, or the second emergence of Babylon around 600 B.C., in her magnificence, is still talked about, with her hanging gardens that many consider one of the great wonders of the world. The great walled city built by Nebuchadnezzar, who later attacked Judah and carried the Jews off, was considered impregnable. The city was so tightly secured that the people had absolutely no fear of ever being attacked, destroyed, or overtaken. [11]

The Prophet Daniel in Babylon

The prophet Daniel prophesied during the time of the Babylonian captivity of the Jews, when the Babylonians had carried them off to Babylon. God had given him a revelation of the world empires that would succeed from the time of the Babylonian era all the way until the end of time.

During a dream he saw the world empires represented in a giant figure. The body parts of the statue represented each successive kingdom that was to arise. The head of the figure, which was made of gold, represented Babylon; then came the shoulders and chest made of silver, representing Medo-Persia; the hips made of Bronze, representing Greece; and finally the legs made of iron, corresponding to Rome. The feet were made of iron and clay, which relates to the last stages of the Roman Empire (Daniel 2:31-42).

The world empires Daniel saw in the vision of the figure he saw again later in another vision, only in the later vision, the empires were depicted to him as animals or beasts (Daniel 7:3-7).

The Beasts

Daniel saw Babylon as a lion, Medo-Persia as a bear, Greece as a leopard, and Rome he saw different than all the rest, a beast that had ten horns. These ten horns corresponded to the ten toes of the feet in the first vision of world empires represented by the statue (Daniel 7:4-7).

When the Jews were carried off to Babylon, strange things began to happen to their customs and traditions. Prior to their captivity, the Jews had been given the Law of God in the Ten Commandments and various other statutes at Mount Sinai. These regulations were God's plan for how Israel was to be governed. God's regulations covered every aspect of their life. Included within the regulations were holidays, customs, and behaviors that were in accordance with the Mosaic Law as passed down in the book of Leviticus. Whether it was the temple purification rites, the concept of the blood atonement wrought through animal sacrifices, or the civic responsibility of the citizens, or even the cultural aspects of their society, the *Law* ruled over all and was the absolute guide of the people. The *Law* was absolute referee, whether for conscience or the state.

The Hebrew nation was truly a peculiar nation, a chosen people different from all the rest. They were set apart from all the Gentile nations, who fashioned their civilizations out of the Nimrodian Babylonian concepts.

The gentile governing powers came from abstract notions about their deities, myths, and lore, that originated from Nimrod's Babylon, the Mother of Harlots. In this remarkable way the world's empires, each arising and succeeding the other until today, have committed acts of immorality, and have become drunk with pagan tradition and worship.

The Babylonians had their gods and goddesses Bel or Bal, as he was called, and Astarte and Ishtar, the goddess from whom comes the present Easter. These are but mere clues as to how the transcendence of the principle of Mystery Babylon effects the world today.

Watered Down Moses

It was, however, during the Babylonian captivity of the Jews, that much of the orthodoxy of the Mosaic Law and it's keeping, began to be undermined and diluted by the culture of the pagan Babylonian Empire and its pervasive influence.

In Babylon the Jews began to exercise the oral tradition over and above the written Law, and without the centerpiece of the faith (the temple), the Jews had no purification rites available. With no blood justification through animal sacrifices, the national conscience of the Jew began to compromise the Law. Special addenda to the literal interpretation of the Law were allowed in an attempt to absolve the national conscience. The oral tradition evolved and then was formalized with the Talmud, which is the written oral tradition. As the national conscience retreated and darkened, the selected people of God also entertained Babylonian Mysticism and the occult.

Babylon the Root of Jewish Mysticism

The influence of Babylonian Mysticism has transcended the ages as the Jews today consult and entertain the Kaballah, which is the Jewish book of the occult. The derivation of the Kaballah was the ancient Nimrodian system, which had been handed down to Babylon during the time of Nebuchadnezzar. In Babylon (the third fallen king) the Jews learned to sin the sin of the pagan nations, which was fornication with the Mother of Harlots.

The Fourth Fallen King - Medo-Persia

In the later part of the sixth century B.C., the ancient history of the near and middle east culminated in the establishment of the Persian Empire (558-330 B.C.) by Cyrus and Darius the Great.

In remote times some Aryan tribes separated themselves from other members of their families and sought new places to dwell on the plateau of Iran. The tribes that settled to the south became known as the Persians, while those that settled in the northwest mountain region became known as the Medes. The names of the two peoples were always closely associated. [12]

The Persians were destined to become the dominant tribe. Eventually the Persian kings ruled over Egypt, Palestine, Syria, Asia Minor, Mesopotamia, Iran and for a time, Northwestern India, and Trace. The empire stretched from the Mediterranean to Central Asia, and from the Black and Caspian Sea to the Persian Gulf and Indian Ocean. [13]

Under Cyrus the Great (who was called the servant of the Lord by Isaiah the prophet some fifty years before Cyrus was even born, Isaiah 45:1) the Medes and the Persians built a vast empire which lasted over 200 years. [14]

The empire, which was centered in Persia and called the Achaemeid Empire, included most of the known world. The Medes and the Persians came to power by the overthrow of the great Babylonian empire. God had told Daniel that this was going to happen, because the Babylonians had gone too far in oppressing the Jews (Isaiah 43:14).

The impregnable city of Babylon was captured by diverting the Euphrates River. The Medes and Persians then entered underneath the great walls through the conduits where the river had watered the city. [15]

The fall of Babylon automatically carried with it a claim to the Babylonian possessions in the west. In both Syria and Palestine, the native peoples welcomed Cyrus as a liberator. He reciprocated by respecting local traditions and religious practices. The Jews of the Exile were permitted to return to Jerusalem and to rebuild the temple. [16]

Persian Art Reveals Mystery Babylon

The Persians and Medes took their ideas of art from the Egyptians and the Babylonians, and they, too, worshipped gods and goddesses of nature; such as the sun, sky and fire. They even believed that their gods had social powers, and so their lives, like those of the great empires before them, were highly controlled by myths. [17]

When Persia invaded Greece in the early 400s B.C., it was the beginning of the end. The Greeks were able to stop the expansion of that empire, and to expel the invaders. Then came Alexander the Great, and in 331 B.C. conquered the Medo-Persian Empire. His empire extended from 323-145 B.C.

The Fifth Fallen King - Greece

During the time period of the Lord Jesus Christ, Rome ruled the world, but Greece ruled the minds of men. Greece was the birthplace of Western Civilization. It was Greece that gave the world Plato and his most famous student, Aristotle. But, advanced as Greece had become in the study of law, medicine, philosophy, and public speaking, they, too, believed that a pantheon of deities watched over them. [18]

The god worshipped in Greece with the name Dionysus, or Bacchus, is expressly identified with Osiris of Egypt, who is, of course, as we have mentioned, Nimrod (according to the great historian Orpheus). [19]

Bacchus is often seen in pictures holding an ivy branch in one hand and a cup in the other. The ivy branch was carried in worship by the devotees of Bacchus bound around their necks, and carried in their hands, or they had the ivy branch indelibly stamped on their bodies. The reason for this was because the name in Greek for ivy was Kissos, and was one of the names of Bacchus. Further, it must be noted, that the name of Cush (who was the father of Nimrod) was properly pronounced Kissioi in Greek. It was through the name Cush that the priests became familiar with the ancient mysteries. Since Kissioi means Cush, then the branch of ivy that was of such prominence in all the Baccanalian ceremonies was an express symbol of Bacchus himself. [20]

Bacchus as the son of Cush, none other than Nimrod, took on the name of his father Kissos, the Greek for ivy. In fact, he was even called *The Real Branch*. One of the names of the Messiah, as expressed in the book of Isaiah was exactly that name, *The Branch*. Attributing the name of the son of God to a pagan deity is utmost blasphemy, and so the cup in the hand of the Great Harlot of Revelation that is full of blasphemous names can be seen in the Greek worship of Bacchus, or old Nimrod. The relationship of the Greek religion to the ancient Babylonian Nimrod comes through clearly. [21]

Can the multitude of names attributed to Nimrod, in symbolic form, and from empire to empire, be anything other than the names that fill the cup of the Harlot that sits on top of the seven-headed and ten-horned beast of Revelation 17:3, 4?

> And he carried me away in the Spirit into a wilderness; and I saw a *woman* sitting on a scarlet beast, full of blasphemous names, having seven heads and ten horns. And the woman was clothed in purple and scarlet, and adorned with gold and precious stones and pearls, having in her hand *a gold cup full of abominations and of the unclean things of her immorality*.
>
> Revelation 17:3, 4
> (emphasis mine)

Nimrod's Babylon is the Mother of Harlots that has deceived the whole world, even to this day. For example, the Christianizing of pagan holidays that have come to be known as Easter (worship of Astarte) and Christmas (Birth of Nimrod, son of Cush).

Very briefly, the first five world empires that are mentioned in Revelation 17 as having fallen, which correspond to the first five heads of the Beast, have been put forth. Where they all came from has been explained, along with how they were shaped and influenced by their mother, Nimrod's Mystery Babylon, the Mother of Harlots.

To recap, here they are again in their ascending order through time:

1. Egypt
2. Assyria
3. Babylon
4. Medo-Persia
5. Greece

And they are seven kings; *five have fallen, ONE IS,*
Revelation 17:10
(emphasis mine).

The sixth kingdom upon which the Harlot sits is...Rome.

Chapter Eleven

ROME
THE SIXTH EMPIRE

T he empire that was begun according to tradition by the twin brothers, Romulus and Remus, two shepherd boys, grew from a small community of sheep herders to an enormous empire of over seventy million people. The city was situated next to the Tiber River atop seven hills, and far enough inland that it was protected from marauding bands of pirates. These natural barriers protecting the city enabled Rome to grow over the centuries, and become the sixth empire of the world. [1]

Its beginnings date back to 735 B.C., and by 275 B.C. it controlled most of the Italian peninsula. Rome peaked at about A.D. 100 and fell in A.D. 476. During its peak it extended as far north as the British Isles and as far east as Persia. Rome was the capital city of the Roman Empire, and was inhabited by over two million people at its height. The glue that held the empire together was the Pax Romana, or the Roman peace. [2]

The peace was maintained by a huge army that continued to grow as immigrants trickled into the empire, and many were recruited into the military. The army had 300,000 men.

The Roman law was the rule enforced by the might and strength of the military, which brought this peace. Although Republican institutions of government were kept throughout the history of the empire, it was the emperors who held absolute rule. They nominated the cousuls and appointed new senators. The citizens' assemblies had little power. Emperors also headed the army and directed the making of the law. The authority of the Roman emperor overruled any act of the Senate. [3]

The Romans worshipped an emperor after his death as a god, similar to the Egyptian worship of the pharaoh. It was emperor worship which provided for a common base of loyalty throughout the empire. The Romans adopted the worship of the Greeks. They believed that the gods controlled nature, but they changed the names of the Greek gods to Roman names. The emperors were the supreme voice of the land under their superstitious submission to the pagan gods. [4]

Although much great romantic literature has been written about Rome, the prophet Daniel saw it as a ferocious beast, and spoke of Rome in more violent terms than all the rest of the world empires that had come before it (Daniel 7:7).

It was a restless kingdom that was not content with its size, and continually overwhelmed new areas of land and peoples. Perhaps the reason for its fall in A.D. 476 was due to its own weight.

The Roman Empire must be remembered for the fact that it relished the spectacle of organized murder in the gladiatorial games where men actually died for the amusement and enjoyment of the emperor and the populace. It was also for great sport that Christians were fed to lions. But foremost, Rome must be remembered for being the sixth great empire of the world, and murderer of the King of kings. What an epitaph! It was the empire the apostle John wrote of when he said, "five have fallen, *ONE IS,*" (Revelation 7:10 emphasis mine).

Chapter Twelve

THE SEVENTH HEAD

And he stood on the sand of the seashore. And I saw a beast coming up out of the sea, having ten horns and seven heads, and on his horns were ten diadems, and on his heads were blasphemous names.
                                        Revelation 13:1

Historical ignorance creates a blindness, blocking the ability to gaze into the prophetic future. This is especially true for the average North American citizen. If one cannot see where he has come from, he certainly will not see where he is going. When it comes to a knowledge of world history, not just Americans, but Christians as well, have very little understanding of the past. The same is true when it comes to a grasp of the history of their own country.

But of greater significance and perplexity is the historical blindness inherent within the great theologians and spiritual leaders of the North American church. Their willingness to be coaxed along in a red blooded nationalism seems to blind them to a truly objective understanding of who we Americans are and where we came from.

American Roots

When it comes to an understanding of Great Britain, the mother country, Americans are totally in the dark. America has become ingrown and isolated from the world by her tremendous wealth and the great oceans that surround her like a moat. These factors have created a corporate aloofness that insulates the nation from the rest of the world. Most Americans simply do not care about historic facts relating to their own national identity.

As the world stampedes toward a One-World System and a New World Order, Americans must not loose sight of their European roots lest they lose their clear Christian world view and become totally disoriented.

Since America was founded and established by Europeans, namely refugees from Great Britain, there should be knowledge of the mother country. The essence of the American spirit began at it's creation by the corporate soul of the forefathers who came from Great Britain.

Great Britain

The history of Great Britain is that of how a small island off the mainland of Europe grew to become the world's most powerful empire. Not only during the time of its own existence, but in all of history there has not been a world empire like the British Empire. [1]

It was the industrial revolution of the 1700s that made Britain the world's richest manufacturing country, and after 1815, the city of London became the Vatican of world banking. [2] The empire was so enormous it was said that the sun never set on it. By 1799 the empire covered about a fourth of the world's land, and about a fourth of its people. [3]

Since people generally do not like to speak in disparaging terms concerning their own heritage, it is difficult to lay bare the truth of the British Empire without bringing offense, nevertheless, there are important hidden facts that need to come forth about the British Empire in order to see clearly the fulfillment of biblical prophecy.

When the British Empire is spoken of, what types of thoughts come up in the mind of the English speaking people? What was the British Empire? *Is it possible that the British Empire is represented by the seventh head of the Beast of Revelation chapter 13?* What was behind this Christian appearing empire?

. In searching world history since the time of the fall of the Roman Empire, there has not arisen another world empire except the British Empire.

The apostle John saw a vision while exiled on the Isle of Patmos (90 A.D.). In symbolic form, John saw a beast coming up out of the sea. It had seven heads and ten horns. Six of these heads have already been identified in the preceding chapters, and now, as history is searched since the fall of the sixth head, Rome, there has come another world empire, the <u>British Empire</u>. "And they are seven kings; five have fallen, one is, *the other has not yet come.*" (Revelation 17:10, emphasis mine).

But for some strange reason, neither North American nor Northern European theologians have even considered the emergence and existence of the British Empire as the fulfillment of the seventh head of the Beast. The fact is, the British Empire is the only world empire since the fall of Rome, and so the only possible fulfillment.

The amazing power of this truly vast world-wide empire did not reach its zenith and its true status as undisputed ruler of the earth until Napoleon was defeated at the Battle of Waterloo in 1815. When the British finally conquered the French, it can be said that the British Empire ruled the world for about one hundred years, from 1815 until the outbreak of WWI. [4]

The Global Rule

The British Empire in 1815, the seventh imperial head of John's Beast, emerged as supreme power over the area that encompassed the old Roman Empire.

However, while the empire increased in power, it was specifically accruing to the revenues of The City under the crown, not to England itself. (The city of London fell under the control of an elite group of bankers-*the Rothschilds*. More explanation of this international elite will be given shortly.) [5]

The City today controls over 80% of all international business transactions. England itself was bled dry by the hidden government, and was harnessed for the special aims of The City, which became the seat for an International One World Government. [6]

The Internationalists (the bankers) have no feeling of nationalism or patriotism towards any nation, including England. England, once Christian controlled to a degree, under the influence of the Protestant Reformation, fell under the power of mammon, controlled by the international money cabal (the Rothschilds). [7]

Note--This is not to dismiss the important workings of the Holy Spirit in England during those times. God did profound things in the 18th and 19th centuries in England. The religious zealots that founded the United States were people who came from Britain and had a deep orthodox knowledge of the Scriptures. But the secular English state tried to control the operation of the true church, and this became intolerable for true believers; this was one of the key motivating issues for their exodus to the new world.

The East India Company

Little, if any, is known in the Western Hemisphere of the nefarious ways in which the British Empire gained its supremacy over the earth. But the peoples of India and China can give grim testimony to the most notorious of all the terrible machines of conquest that the Empire possessed, the infamous East India Company. [8]

The company was formed in 1600 when, following the defeat of the Spanish Armada, Queen Elizabeth granted a charter to certain London based merchants to trade in the East,. The company grew stronger as it became ensconced in worldwide trade. It was allowed to have monopolistic privileges in return for a fraction of its earnings, and so it gained tremendous financial might. As it grew, it built a large private army which contested with the French and Dutch traders, and learned methods of control and looting in India. Great control came over India by bribery and graft as the company set up a puppet government which then imposed forced sales of merchandise, and outright looting through tax collecting. If the people resisted, various methods of compulsion were practiced, such as fines, imprisonment, and floggings, forcing the people to submit. [9]

The British taxed the people to exhaustion, and when famine conditions arose in 1770 due to poor weather, ten million people in Bengal starved to death. [10]

East India House

Towards the end of the 17th century when America's war for independence from the iron-like grip of British dominion was succeeding, the political circles associated with the British East India Company *seized nearly complete control over British political party affairs*. The historical significance of this event, and its subsequent effect on world affairs has been monumental, and yet completely neglected in this hemisphere. [11]

A new prime minister came on the scene in one William Petty. At that time Petty negotiated the peace treaty with the U.S.A. (after the war for independence), and also directed British intelligence services in a complex world wide task of conquest and subversion. Even though the American Revolution had succeeded, in the eyes of this man, it was not the end of the effort to subjugate the American colonies to British control. [12]

Over in India a board of control for the affairs of India was set up under the leadership of one Henry Dundus. It was Dundus who controlled the Indian operation for 30 years, during which time he proposed that Indian opium be poured into China as an instrument of war and looting (sound familiar?). Dundus was also the man to whom Aaron Burr, Vice President to Jefferson, reported in England.

In 1787 Dundus wrote a master plan to extend the opium traffic into China, and personally supervised the world-wide traffic of opium which had been escalated by the East India Company. [13]

General Cornwallis, the British general who surrendered at Yorktown, was reassigned after the war by Dundus to be commander-in-chief and Governor General over India. Britain was gearing up for a military offensive over all Asia. Finally, in 1803, the British East India Company subdued and controlled the entire subcontinent of Asia. The army had now swelled to over a quarter-million men, with a navy patrolling the seas from the southwest Pacific to the Persian Gulf. This power engaged in conflict after conflict, inflicting fatalities in the millions. [14] But people in the Western Hemisphere are routinely ignorant of such facts of history.

To further loot India the British raised high tariffs, but kept India open for British goods. India paid for its imported goods from Britain by opium from plantations developed by the British. The opium was sold to the Chinese to not only oppress them, but to raise money to pay for the British goods sold to India. [15]

The peasantry, which were those who cultivated cotton, were treated with the most savage and revolting actions. They were subjected to torture, and every effort, lawful or unlawful, to extract revenues. When they tried to run away from this brutal treatment they were rounded up by the British, flogged, and put back to work. As the nation's cotton began to disappear due to this kind of treatment, the exploiters looked to American slave cotton as a viable alternative source of cheap raw material. [16]

The British occupation of India was maintained and manipulated by a cunningly devised cultural warfare. The idea for maintaining control was to prevent any and all importation of Western ideals or values into Western India. [17] The East India Company patronized and advanced the most outrageous aspects of the pagan Indian religions, and made Hinduism and Islam British state run religions.

When the British finally turned their gaze upon America, the technique they used was to displace Western Christian beliefs of the American people by importing and introducing Eastern Indian religious beliefs, thus undermining Western values. The drug wars can also be traced to the East India House strategy. [18]

"To destroy a country," Solzhenitsyn wrote, "you must first cut its roots." If America's roots are in the Judeo-Christian values and traditions, they have in large measure been severed. Today, of course, the root base of the philosophy of the New Age is directly taken from Indian Hinduism.

John Stuart Mill

The chief intelligence officer of the Company into the 1900s was John Stuart Mill, who ran the evil organization from London. When the Indians revolted in 1857, the atrocities of that conflagration so outraged the world that Queen Victoria stepped in, and within a few years the East India Company was dissolved, but the industrious John Stuart Mill turned his attention to the fledgling nation of America. He was ready to apply the knowledge gained from his many years of experience in India to the conquest of America. [19]

Before we delve into the subversion of America by the Company, it must also be said that the East India House in London became the central point of interaction and dialogue for the main antagonists of Western civilization. This central location became the seat of the existential writers that focused on a theology of man as the center of all things. The propagators of this Anglicized Hinduism were men like Henry David Thoreau and Ralph Waldo Emerson. Charles Darwin was also contemporary with these men, and associated with them at the East India House. Their doctrine was the philosophical base from which world-wide cultural warfare would be launched. [20]

The advancement of the New Age movement can actually be traced directly to this think tank operated in London at the East India House run by John Stuart Mill, the oppressor of India. [21] These men did not believe in the creed of all men being created equal, but quite the contrary, that all men by nature were created unequal, and that some were meant to rule, and others to be ruled over. They saw the biblical definition of man submitted to a sovereign Lord God as repugnant to their dreams of globalism. Empire building, in their thinking, began with a definition of man as central, and from that point all considerations would proceed. The colonies in America, which were becoming more and more prosperous under the biblical theology of man, had to be finally conquered and brought under control. [22]

Government and Man's Nature

The American Constitution was built upon a foundation that had its roots in a biblical definition of man. The writers of it viewed man as having fallen from a divine position with God. They saw that man had became corrupted with a sin nature. Since absolute objectivity could not be possessed by one man, due to his fallen nature, the Founding Fathers developed the Constitution very carefully. They placed checks and balances into the structure of the government. There were to be three branches of the federal government: Executive, Judicial, and Legislative. Each branch was to insure that no one man or group of men could gain absolute power; each branch would balance the others. Tantamount in their minds was the cruelty of despotism; the absolutism of one sovereign ruler from which they had fled when they left England.

The framers of the Constitution had a keen sense of British history when they sat down to write the Constitution. They clearly had in mind the historical facts of the evolution of the monarchial system in England.

The Monarchial System

When Henry VIII became King of England in the 16th century he was already wed to Catherine of Aragon. When he wanted to divorce her and wed Anne Boleyn, it caused a separation between Henry and the Pope. The Roman Catholic Church refused to sanction the marriage. Nevertheless, King Henry went on with the marriage and was ex-communicated from the Roman Catholic Church. Henry then ordered the English Parliament to declare the King as the supreme head of the Roman Catholic Church of England.

The separation of the Church of England from Rome effectively brought the Protestant Reformation to England. In 1534, by Henry's insistence, Parliament passed two acts that made the break complete. The first declared that the Pope had no authority in England. The second declared the Church of England a separate institution with the King as its head (The famous *Supremacy Act.*). Both church and state had come under the authority of the King.

It was this act by King Henry VIII, bringing the religious and secular under one roof, that eventually led to the reasoning behind the first amendment of the United States Constitution. The spirit of that amendment and its intent was not to eliminate religion from its influence on government, but quite the contrary, to keep government out of religion.

Later, both Henry's son and Queen Elizabeth caused the work of establishing the Church to go forward. Upon the arrival of the 1600s, England was ready to embark on a great era of development.

When England defeated the Spanish Armada in 1588 through the leadership of Sir Francis Drake, she had become the undisputed ruler of the seas. She now controlled all the shipping lanes, exacting tribute for maritime activities from all of Europe.

The last piece of contrivance for realization of a Global World Empire was the ability to subjugate nations of the world through the sheer power of capital and credit.

The Battle of Waterloo

The opportunity for the seizure of mammon arose during Napoleon's attempt to seize Europe after the French Revolution at the famous Battle of Waterloo. How was the Battle of Waterloo utilized to further the aims of those who sought for a New World Order? [23]

The French Revolution

First it must be understood that the real force of the French Revolution was not a spontaneous explosion within the corporate breast of the collective lower class of France. Historians have long blamed the masses for the revolution. However, enough facts have come to light to prove that France was infiltrated by subversives of the Internationalists to destabilize her into a chaotic mass. Why was France selected as the beginning of the global revolution for one-worldism? [24] The Internationalists based in England saw in France a formidable opponent to the aims of the centralization of European Capital. [25] France had to be destabilized into chaos. Then, with the all important defeat of Napoleon, the opportunity arose to seize financial power in the hands of the money conspiracy. While the philosophical intrigue and planning to upset the unifying aspects of monarchial family intermarriage shifted temporarily to center on Bavaria and the

German states, [26] the war chest of world revolution was being concentrated and built in London. [27]

The Rothschilds Seize Control

Here is how it occurred. Upon the Battle of Waterloo hung the future of the European continent. If Napoleon were successful, France would be the undisputed master of Europe. If Napoleon were defeated, England would reign supreme. [28]

Obviously, the success of Lord Wellington would have tremendous positive implications on the British stock exchange. With Nathan Rothschild positioned in London, the headquarters of the Rothschild banking dynasty, the stage was set for the soon to be financial rulers of the nations. As the armies closed in for the battle, the secret agents of the Rothschilds gathered the information to whisk back to London. [29]

When the outcome of the battle was known to Nathan Rothschild, he gave the signal and his people began quietly selling consuls on the stock market. As the consuls began to pour onto the market, it created a stampede that caused the market to fall, and then cascade into a panic selloff. It was feared that Napoleon had won the battle and Rothschild was privy to this information. [30]

Unbeknownst to those outside his circle, Rothschild was manipulating the market downward so that he could buy up the consuls at five cents on the dollar. When the news hit that the British actually defeated Napoleon, the market soared like an eagle, and Rothschild and his banking kingdom had seized, in one day, the vast war chest for the economic control of the nations. [31]

The Rothschilds were of Jewish descent, and England, being a Christian nation, was not inclined to allow Jews into positions of political decision making. Rothschild's response to this racist policy was this, "I care not for the laws of the nations. Give me the wealth of the nations and I'll make the laws." [32]

Bank of England

With this in mind, we must backtrack through English history to the year 1694. This was the year the Bank of England, a privately owned bank called the *Central Bank*, was established. The establishing of the Bank of England was of no small importance in world history. It was utilized to advance the power of the City of London, hence, the entire affairs of the rapidly growing British Empire. [33]

When Rothschild pulled off his seizure of the British economic system, he also gained control of the Bank of England and the City of London. With the demise of France, and the English victory over Napoleon at Waterloo, England in 1815 emerged as the undisputed ruling power of Europe. The power of mammon was now in their grasp, the monarchial headship was removed, the influence of the Church of England was minimized in state affairs, and all state matters were subjugated to the Barons of Finance.

Chapter Thirteen

THE INNATE DRIVE

And I saw one of his heads as if it had been slain, and his fatal wound was healed. And the whole earth was amazed and followed after the Beast.
Revelation 13:3

Profound events were taking place that were setting the stage for the death of the empire by a blow of war.

Behind the Internationalist's drive towards a One-World Government is a strange, innate sense of humanitarianism. It's as though the mandate to convert the world to a global village is their providential lot. It is the same drive that *Cain* had when he offered to God a sacrifice of vegetables, man's human effort to right his conscience due to Adam's transgression. Globalism is the epitome of man's effort to bring about peace. The Globalists seek to do this through the unification of the earth, but their determination is to do it strictly through human means. The philosophy for bringing this about is through the dialectic of *the ends justify the means*, or *whatever it takes to get the job done*. If it means trashing a human here or a nation there, whatever the cost, it must be paid. This is the rationale of the dialectic of those seeking the global revolution and A New World Order.

The Internationalist's Apparatus

The Internationalists seek the humanitarian goal of world peace and safety. Their goals seem noble and virtuous. Because of this few question their motives. The means for pulling off this humanitarian extravaganza is quite another story. Ironically, the Internationalists use the device of war as a means to peace.

The Money Machine

The Internationalists will always profit from war because it doubly indentures a nation. First, it causes a nation to borrow in order to build its war machine; and second, the nation has to borrow again after the war to rebuild it's infrastructure.

The creation of nuclear weapons also serves the interest of the money powers. Nations that would dare to think of a debt moratorium, or repudiation, are brought back into tow by the threat of nuclear attack. Nuclear weapons are the ultimate collection agency tool.

Chapter Fourteen

WORLD WARS I AND II

When America's industrial might was harnessed by the creation of the Federal Reserve System, the mobilization of credit became available to finance a New World Order (See a later chapter on the Federal Reserve). All that needed to be done was to create a world war. Most historians will admit that although there were two world wars, World War I and World War II, they were ostensibly one war with a period of cessation of conflict. They would also admit that beginning World War I had no apparent rationale behind it.

The Archduke of Austria was assassinated, and as a result the whole world went to war. Why? To this day there seems to be no clear answer, unless one sees that the International Bankers had everything to gain by a world war. After all, there would be great profit in making huge loans to so many countries.

The international debt that accumulated after these two wars staggers the imagination. What an incredible money machine! Remember:

The borrower will be slave to the lender.

Proverbs 22:7

The gigantic cash flow off the interest of mega-loans to the nations would be used to create a New World Order. A world order after the pattern suggested by Engels and Karl Marx, whose principles were based upon Adam Weishaupt's Order of the Illuminati. [1]

Woodrow Wilson

Woodrow Wilson, during his second campaign to become President, campaigned under the slogan, "He'll keep us out of the war", but within months of his inauguration he drew America into World War I. America began to borrow heavily to build up its war machine, and finance a war on the other side of the earth. Many purport that Wilson was a pawn in the game of international power and world politics. [2]

The *war to end all wars*, as it was called, served the Internationalists in two ways. One, it brought the world into terrific debt, and two, it prepared the nations to seek peace at any price. War weary and in great debt, the nations were ready to sacrifice on the altar of peace, to a great degree, their national sovereignty.

The League of Nations

A League of Nations was proposed by Woodrow Wilson, which was the first step toward organizing the world into a One World Government. Wilson, who was manipulated by his mentor, Col. House, put forth the plan for the League of Nations in his famous fourteen points. [3]

Wilson's plan for a New World Order was well received by all nations except his own, the United States. Patriotic Americans saw the danger of such a setup and throttled the idea of the League. Wilson failed, and died a broken man. So did the banker's first attempt for A New World Order.

Council on Foreign Relations

The Council on Foreign Relations was created by the Globalists after World War I because of the League's failure. Its purpose was to monitor and determine American foreign policy so that America's decision making with regards to the nations of the world was in step with the ultimate goal of a World Government. The ground work for the C.F.R. was laid by Col. House, who was acting as the Internationalist's agent in America.[4] More will be said in a later chapter on the C.F.R.

The Russian Revolution

During the final years of World War I, the Russian Revolution was carefully planned and tried. The Bolsheviks trained in New York, were financed by the International Kuen Loeb & Company, a New York banking house, and were sent through Germany into Russia to overthrow the Czar.[5]

The Bolsheviks were aided by Max Warburg, who was brother to Paul Warburg, the architect of the Federal Reserve. Max was in control of the German banking system.[6]

But why bring about the perfect neo-feudal state *in Russia first*? The plotters had several reasons: It was the largest land mass between Europe and Asia, and the outbreak of Globalism as a system could be more easily managed. Its population was large enough to mobilize and most easily conquerable. Its technology was lagging and its financial power was easily assailable.

The setup for Globalism in its final form would begin in Russia, but its conception and financing were formulated by the banking elite of Europe.[7]

Orchestration of World War II

As the bankers from Wall Street (J.P. Morgan & Co.) moved to rearm Germany, the aspiring Adolf Hitler viewed the Bolshevik revolution, and the attempt for world government through the League of Nations as a Jewish plot to take over the world. He saw the bankers as the principle movers and shakers in this gigantic effort.[8]

The Protocols of the Learned Elders of Zion, a forged document, was cunningly leaked to Hitler by the world planners to make him think the New World Order was a Jewish plot. [9]

Seventh Head Slain

World War II, which actually was a resumption of World War I, was in the mind of the world planners, a necessary evil. The British Empire had to be dissolved.

The great sword that wounded the seventh head of the Beast was the two world wars that brought the seventh head, the British Empire, to an end. After World War II, the British Empire ceased, but it should be carefully noted that the seat of global financial power remained in London, unscathed by war. In fact, the money powers became more powerful, due to the massive indebtedness the wars created.

In the Bible it is asked, "Who is able to wage war with the Beast?" (Revelation 13:4). Yet the seventh empire was killed by the sword of war. What entity, what government, what other opponent out there could launch a conflict against the seventh head? When it can be seen how World War I and World War II were orchestrated by the International Bankers, who had no allegiance to England or the British Empire, but merely used them for their purposes in accomplishing a Global World Empire, the question is answered. The seventh head was slain by a sword of its own creation. [10]

Chapter Fifteen

THE GREAT SWORD

Enter Hitler

Hitler's Third Reich was supported and built by international capital, much of it coming from Wall Street as the Internationalists prepared the world for another bath of blood, and another round of debt. [1]

The need for the resumption of conflict was evident in that without the U.S.A. in the League of Nations, a World Government was impossible. What was needed was more debt and more cries for *peace, peace.* Hence the war needed to be rekindled.

When Hitler arose and began to foment such vehement hatred toward the Jews, it was because he saw that a group of Jewish bankers had seized control of the world banking system. He failed to see that the small group of bankers also included

Gentile banking houses. [2] Germany's woes were not the fault of world Jewry.

Hitler blamed the whole of Jewry for the heavy-handed shackles of the Treaty of Versailles which ended WWI. From his view, Germany was in ruins due to the Jews.

Hitler's Hatred Manipulated

Then Hitler's hatred was enflamed by the falsified document of *The Protocols of the Learned Elders of Zion..* [3] This document was allegedly smuggled into Germany, and was widespread amongst the German people. The document was meant to be construed by the Germans as a Jewish blueprint for a New World Order. The document in form is almost identical to the 18th century *Protocols of the Illuminati*. That there is some ongoing conspiracy seems without doubt. That there are some Jews involved is unquestionable. That there is a Jewish conspiracy is highly *improbable*.

Hitler incriminated a whole race because one handful of people of Jewish descent, joined a number of Gentile bankers to plunge the whole world into a sea of red ink. There were multitudes of Jews living throughout Europe that were vehemently against a Jewish state. They were anti-Zionistic and opposed a state for the Jews. They argued that until Messiah comes there should not be a place for the Jews. Until their King had come there should be no kingdom.

Because of the secrecy that has enshrouded the International Banking Cabal, it is in truth not known to the mass of Jewry, nor to the rest of the world, for that matter. That this International Banking Elite have a feeling for Israel is clear in that it was the Rothschilds who helped fund the re-establishment of the State of Israel. They were also behind the scenes setting the stage for the Balfour declaration. [4]

Hitler's Reaction to the Jews

There have been those who have claimed that Karl Marx was a Jew. It is true that Marx's family was of Jewish descent, but his parents converted to Protestantism before Karl's birth. [5] The reason for those who falsely claim Marx as a Jew is to add credence to the claim for the Jewish conspiracy theory. Karl Marx was baptized Protestant. Later in his life Marx turned from God and developed a hatred toward religion in any form. Marxism was atheistic, denying the God of Judaism as well as the God of Christianity.

It was Karl Marx who instigated the philosophy of Communism that was so deleterious towards Germany's nation building in the 1850s and 60s. It is also true, however, in all fairness, that in the Russian Revolution there were apostate Jews who hated religion, but had a politico-Zionism at heart. It is true that at the helm of the finances for this global world rule were the Rothschilds (formerly the Bauers) who were of Jewish background. This is what Hitler saw. [6]

Hitler's diabolical hatred of the Jews stemmed from his perceptions that the Jews as a people sought to take over the whole world, and the Rothschild financed Bolshevik Revolution was another step toward that end. In many of his speeches he expressed this belief.

The following is from a German newspaper:

> On February 24, 1920, an ex-corporal in the German army named Adolf Hitler, and a group of professional anti-semitic agitators, including Julius Streicher, Alfred Rosenberg, and Gottfried Feder, met in a Munich beer hall and founded a new National Socialist Party.

The core of their National Socialist (Nazi) Party program was the racist doctrine that only he in whose veins German blood flows might be considered a citizen of Germany, and therefore no Jew could belong to the German nation. The Nazis declared that anti-Semitism was the emotional foundation of their movement; every member of the Nazi party was an anti-Semite.

Hitler, the Fuehrer, or dictatorial leader, of the Nazi Party, proudly announced his anti-Semitism, as well as his inhumanity.

> Yes we are barbarians; we want to be barbarians; it is an honorable title. We shall rejuvenate the world; this world is near it's end. . . .We are now near the end of the Age of Reason. . . .The Ten Commandments have lost their validity. Conscience is a Jewish invention. It is a blemish, like circumcision. . .There is no such thing

as truth, either in the moral or in the scientific sense. We must distrust the intelligence and the conscience and must place our trust in our instincts. . . .And was not the whole doctrine of Christianity, with its faith in redemption, its moral code, its conscience, its conception of original sin, the outcome of Judaism? [7]

This last statement of Hitler's is the most revealing about the global conspiracy as he felt it related to the Jews.

The struggle for world domination will be fought between us; between Germans and Jews.

Adolf Hitler [8]

Hitler's own attempt at world dominion was essentially an attempt to break out of the grasp of the International Banking Elite.

Chapter Sixteen

THE SATANIC RESURRECTION

And I saw one of his heads as if it had been slain, and his fatal wound was healed. And the whole earth was amazed and followed after the Beast.
Revelation 13:3

Here in the 13th chapter of Revelation there is a resurrection of the seventh head which had been slain. The resurrection is actually mentioned three times. In the 17th chapter of Revelation the resurrection is also mentioned.

And the beast which was and is not, is himself also an eighth, and is one of the seven.
Revelation 17:11

These Scriptures must be looked at together. How can chapter 13 show seven heads where the seventh is slain by a great sword and comes back to life, while in chapter 17 the resurrection of the seventh head is spoken of as an eighth, which comes out of the seven? Why didn't the Holy Spirit, who inspires all Scripture, say something like this? "I looked and saw the seventh head resurrected," and leave it at that? Why does he say in Revelation 17, "I saw an eighth head, which is of the seven." What does this mean? Herein we witness the beauty and precision of the Word of God. There can be only one answer to this question.

When the seventh head's fatal wound is healed it comes back in a *different capacity* or *expanded form*. How can the totality of the Beast as represented by John's panoramic vision of the seven heads and ten horns in Revelation 13 be concentrated into an eighth head? "And the beast which was and is not, is himself also an eighth, and is one of the seven," (Revelation 17:11) It is because this eighth Global World Empire is the synthesis and totality of all the preceding empires combined and concentrated into one head, the eighth head.

In the past, many theologians and others believed that the slain head was a man. During the sixties many thought that John Kennedy would perhaps have a satanic resurrection, and be the revived head or the Antichrist. But it is clear that the heads on the Beast are empires, and these empires are depicted in symbolic form.

The mystery of this Scripture has stumped biblical scholars for centuries. Most of the information that has been missing to solve this mystery was given in the last chapter, but there are some additional facts.

The death blow had to occur to fulfill prophecy. It was necessary for there to be a breakup of the limited world control by the British Empire. It is highly unlikely that the world planners anticipated the degree to which Hitler got out of hand. Certainly the war worked to their advantage, because it ended British world control. It took two world wars to do it.

The Satanic Resurrection

Warfare, specifically global world war, benefits greatly the money brokers, because they derive terrific economic advantage by the financing of both the military build-up, and of the urban renewal projects that come as a result of war's devastation. When the warring factions face the prospects of rebuilding their countries, large sums of money must be borrowed at usurious interest rates, thus bringing in great revenues to the International Bankers. [1]

In this way money is further concentrated in the hands of a banking elite, and the nations are weakened and brought into submission through debt usury. By instigating the wars, and then backing both sides, the bankers can't possibly lose.

> How you have fallen from heaven, O star of the morning, son of the dawn! You have been cut down to the earth, you who have weakened the nations!
>
> Isaiah 14:12

Most historians agree that the two World Wars of this century were actually one great war with several years of peace separating the two parts. If one were to study the elements that forged the beginning of World War I, it would be difficult to find a reason for the whole world to go to war. The fact of the matter is that there was no real cause for a world war to begin in 1914. Why then a war?

There were some interesting problems in Europe prior to the outbreak of hostilities in 1914. Europe could not afford to go to war simply because there was not enough mobilization of credit to enable the funding of the massive buildup necessary to finance such a venture.

The bankers in London solved the problem by contriving to set up a central banking system for the United States. Their agent Paul Warburg had been sent to develop the plan and have it formalized into law. The actual plan came to pass and became known as the Federal Reserve Act. [2] Late in 1913 the United States Congress passed this act, which Woodrow Wilson rubber stamped, centralizing the bank of the United States of America, and thus mobilizing the credit of the industrial giant. This mobilization of credit established the loaning ability to finance the First World War.

Eventually the great World Wars would bring to an end the seventh head of John's Beast, the British Empire. It was slain by a great sword, the World Wars. Out of this would come the resurrected eighth head of the Beast, the final world empire.

Here is the mind which has wisdom. The seven heads
are seven mountains on which the woman sits, and
they are seven kings; five have fallen, one is, the other
has not yet come; and when he comes, he must remain
a little while. And the beast which was and is not, is
also himself an eighth, and is one of the seven, and he
goes to destruction.

Revelation 17:9-11

The Great Miracle Worker

The resurrection of the slain head occurs by the work of the
second Beast, or the *False Prophet*. The False Prophet resurrects
the seventh head. He is the builder of the last great world empire,
which would have ten horns, as spoken of by Daniel. The apostle
John also saw ten horns on his Beast. These horns are ten kings
or kingdoms and correspond to the eighth head (Daniel 7:24).

It is the work of the second Beast to build these kings
together to form the Beast power of a Global World Empire. In
order for there to be an eighth head, the second Beast must be
present and working, since it is through his effort that the New
World Order will arise.

Chapter Seventeen

THE AGENT OF ANTICHRIST

For two thousand years Bible scholars have studied and wondered at the images of the two Beasts of the 13th chapter of the book of Revelation. Throughout the centuries countless attempts have been made to identify each of these symbols as they relate to human history. As we move toward the end of this century, which makes approximately two thousand years since the birth of Christ, and some six thousand years of recorded human history, most all the earth is expecting some kind of climactic event that will usher in the new millennium.

Since believers in Christ look for His imminent return, those within the commonwealth of faith should be watching carefully. The unfolding of events will point to a clear understanding of what, and who, these symbolic creatures represent. The arising of both Beasts are signs that precede the return of Jesus Christ. The believer should be awake and looking intently to bolster his precious faith.

The faithful are charged to warn the world of the judgement, and to open the eyes of the blind with the good news of the salvation of God in Christ. God intended His prophetic word to shine in the darkness, enabling the lost to see clearly the approaching of the *Day of the Lord*. With this call to evangelism, the true disciples of Christ should be keen students of biblical prophecy.

The Common Market

Since the end of the Second World War, with the accompanying end of the British Empire, (the kingdom slain by the sword) unwittingly the world watched as the eighth head, an eighth kingdom, known as the European Common Market, has emerged like a Phoenix from the ashes of the ancient Roman Empire.

In the post World War II beginnings of this entity there were only three countries involved. They were known as BENELUX, or Belgium, Netherlands and Luxemburg. Soon the organization grew to six members, then ten. The entity was to be limited to ten countries according to the original charter. As of this writing there are twelve countries involved.

The Scripture points out that this eighth head or empire will have ten kings or kingdoms combined in an alliance, and they will give their support to a world dictator. The Scripture teaches that this world dictator will be the False Christ, or the Antichrist (Daniel 7:7).

Most of the North American church is well aware of this revived Roman Empire and is watching developments in Europe with great anticipation. As the Common Market advances toward greater unification in 1993, and events change rapidly in Eastern Europe, the anticipation has become more pronounced.

As believers rivet their attention on these most recent developments, however, they seem to be missing a most important fact of Revelation 13. There are *two* Beasts, mentioned in this very important section of Scripture, that appear at the end of the age.

The first Beast is, of course, the seven-headed, ten-horned Beast. The second Beast is little talked about or understood. What about this second Beast? It has been a mystery and lurked in the shadow of the first Beast for thousands of years! Yet it appears at the end of the age along with the global empire of the first Beast.

Few realize that it is the two-horned Beast that is not only contemporary with the final stage of the first Beast, but it is actually the Agent of Antichrist, and the Architect (supercharger) of the Beast System.

If the rising of a One-World Government epicentered in a revived Roman Empire in Europe (Common Market) can be seen, then the second Beast must be in existence and operating, since it is he who is putting it all together. It is the second beast whose function it is to advance, and build the system (the Beast) of Satan. The question remains, who is, and what is, pulling this all together? Who, or what is, this second Beast of Revelation 13:11?

Chapter Eighteen

THE FALSE PROPHET
(THE SECOND BEAST)

There are some hidden clues which emerge from study-ing the first Beast which begin to unlock the identity of the second Beast. A return to a view of the first Beast is vital in discovering these facts.

As most students of prophecy already know, the first Beast of Revelation is also mentioned in Daniel, chapters 7 & 8.. There is a significant difference, however, between what Daniel saw in his vision and what the apostle John saw in his. Both saw a One-World Government, but in the difference between what they saw lies the first key to understanding the second Beast.

Daniel's Vision

Daniel had a preview of world history from his time all the way to the end of the world. He saw the last phase or manifestation of the Beast, which was to be composed of ten kings, or kingdoms (Daniel 7:7).

He also saw a *little horn*, or king, with human eyes (Daniel 7:8). Daniel actually had a preview of the man of lawlessness, or the Antichrist. The Antichrist is also known as the world dictator who will control the ten nation confederacy. So, Daniel saw from his time forward all the way to the last Global World Empire ruled by a man, the Antichrist.

John's View

John, on the other hand, saw panoramically. John, who lived in the first century, was given a total panoramic historic world view of the Beast System beginning with the Egyptian Empire (around 3500 B.C.) all the way through time to the last days, when the ten-horned kingdom of Daniel shows up (the Common Market).

John saw a comprehensive and composite global *world system* that has been under construction over some five thousand years (Revelation 13:1). Daniel saw merely the last form of that system in the last days, with the Antichrist coming to power in the end of time. John in his vision does not give us any view of the Antichrist.

This is not to say that John didn't believe in the Antichrist. He knew of the man of sin, too, but his vision on the Island of Patmos didn't reveal the Antichrist.

Since John saw the first Beast as a system, the pronoun *he* as it pertains to the symbol of the Beast, is not speaking of some person, but rather pertains to the symbol. He, the Beast, the system, not he, the Beast, a man. Contextually this gives us a precedent. The second beast is also a system and not a person, as many have thought. Though the second beast is called the False Prophet, it should not be thought of as an actual human being simply because the pronoun *he* is used. In the case of the second Beast as in the case of the first Beast, the pronoun relates to the symbol.

To bring clarity to the function of the second beast he, or it, has been tagged the False Prophet because this entity gives out a misrepresentation of a religious idea. *Pseudo prophetes* [1] is Greek for false prophet. This simply means false messenger.

Let There Be Clarity

Let there be clarity. First, there will be a man of lawlessness called the Antichrist. Second, there will be the Beast, which is a Global World Governmental system controlled and run by the Antichrist. The Beast is not the Antichrist, and the Antichrist is not the Beast. Third, there will be the False Prophet, or the second beast, which is a system, not a man. The three are distinctive, but they are all related in spirit to serve only one purpose, to bring about the worship of Lucifer on the earth.

The second Beast shows up near the end of time to finalize the construction of the Global World Order (the ten-horned Beast, which is a resurrection of the old Roman Empire, initially epicentered in Europe), and to usher in the man of sin (the Antichrist). He appears on the scene after the healing of a fatal wound to one of the seven heads of the Beast that we see in Revelation 13:3.

The slain head has already been identified as the British Empire. The resurrected head is the developing European Common Market, and the New World Order.

Old Testament Foreshadowings

Old Testament types are always used in the Scripture to foreshadow a New Testament fulfillment. For example, the Ark of the Covenant carried by the Jewish priests was a foreshadowing of the believer. The parting of the Red Sea when God was delivering the Hebrews from Pharaoh was a type of water baptism. The serpent raised in the wilderness was a foreshadowing of the cross. Jesus was the fulfillment of the Old Testament Passover lamb sacrificed by the Jews when they were slaves in Egypt, and so on.

An Old Testament type study of the second Beast of Revelation 13, presents difficulties. The first Beast of Revelation is clearly foreshadowed in Daniel, and John gives more light on the subject, but the second Beast is not so easily seen in the Old Testament. However, there are some clues. John's vision of the first Beast as a system sets the tone for the interpretation of the second Beast as a system also. We must press on to two more clues about the second Beast.

The Two Horns

> Then I saw another beast coming up out of the earth,
> and he had *two horns*.
>
> Revelation 13:11
> (emphasis mine)

Scripture interprets Scripture, and it does not change to suit our conjectural whims. Since the Scripture cannot change and is consistent throughout, if horns represent kings in one place, horns must represent kings in all places throughout apocalyptic Scripture.

> The ram which you saw with *two horns* represents the
> kings of Media and Persia.
>
> Daniel 8:20
> (emphasis mine)

If horns, as has been indicated, represent kings or kingdoms, the Beast with *two horns* in Revelation 13 represents two kings or two kingdoms that combine to make a system that is called the False Prophet.

Although it has been said that there is no clear picture or type in the Old Testament to shed light on the second Beast in Revelation 13, it can be said that the double entente of Media and Persia as a two-horned beast in Daniel 8 does lay down an Old Testament precedent for a two nation confederacy being depicted as a two-horned beast.

Interpreting the False Prophet as a solitary man would not take into consideration the two horns in light of biblical precedents. *The false prophet is an alliance of two kingdoms. It is a system.*

"And he had two horns like a lamb, and he spoke as a dragon" (Revelation 13:11). In the Old Testament, the Scripture as recorded through the prophet Daniel describes the Gentile world powers as beasts. The figurative language of the beasts Daniel uses to describe the ruling powers actually contain the characteristics of those ruling nations. For example, in Daniel's vision he saw the Babylonian empire as a lion, the king of the jungle. This indicated the regal power of Nebuchadnezzar and the greatest of all civilizations. He saw the second empire as a bear, which described the characteristics of the Medes and Persians. The Medo-Persian empire was know for its sheer power and weight in numbers of people. The Greeks were characterized by a leopard, cunning and swift, always stalking his prey and moving quickly over the land. The fourth beast, the Romans, was different than the others. It seemed to be a mechanical and heartless system.

These little cameos of the empires in symbolic form are mentioned here only to bring light and embellishment upon the imagery and nature of the second Beast, or False Prophet.

The Lamb-Likeness of the False Prophet

The second Beast is described as lamb-like in appearance. A lamb in the Bible is first mentioned in the life of Abel (Genesis 4:4). The age old story records that when Abel went to worship the Lord he took a lamb from his flock and sacrificed it to the Lord. This sacrifice was acceptable to the Lord. It represented a type or foreshadowing of the Lord Jesus, the Lamb of God. Again, in the life of Abraham, a lamb was required as a substitutionary sacrifice for his son Isaac when God was testing Abraham's obedience (Genesis 22:8). The ancient Jews were required to sacrifice a lamb, and paint the blood of the lamb on the lintel of the door, escaping the judgement that was coming down on Egypt (Genesis 12:3; Exodus 12: 21-23). In all these cases a lamb was a type, or prefigurement of Christ.

The False Prophet, or the second Beast, is false because it looks Christ-like as a lamb, but in reality it is satanic; it speaks like a dragon. It is a wolf in sheep's clothing.

Remember, this second Beast is a two member confederacy, or system. If the lamb symbol is a Christian symbol, then like it or not the two kingdoms, or horns, represent two Christian nations, or nations that are known as Christian nations. They have a Christian veneer, but underneath it all resides the Devil. The fact that they, or it, speaks as a dragon tells us that underneath that Christian coating is a dragon, the Devil, who is a liar, a thief, and a murderer.

The second beast is two alleged Christian nations joined together to form an alliance, who by their external appearance (looks like a lamb) give out a deceiving message or impression.

What two nations could this be talking about, which have banded together to build a One-World System as the seat of Antichrist? Before this question can be answered there are additional facts that must be brought out.

The Sphere of Authority of the False Prophet

> And he exercises all the authority of the first beast in his presence. And he makes the earth and those who dwell in it to worship the first beast, whose fatal wound was healed.
>
> Revelation 13:12

This section of Scripture is critical in destroying vain speculations concerning the identity of the False Prophet. Hopefully the Scripture itself will lay those annoying conjectures to rest.

The key words are: "he exercises all the authority of the first Beast," (Revelation 13:12). This statement is very revealing. It brings one to ask the very important question, "If the False Prophet exercises all the authority of the first Beast, just what is the extent of that authority?"

The word authority used here is the Greek word *exousia*, which means legislative authority or licensing authority. [2] The False Prophet has all the licensing authority of the first Beast. This is a great deal more than mere religious authority, as we shall see. Just what is the comprehensive authority with which the ten-horned Beast operates?

The Beast with the ten horns, and the seven heads, as you will recall, was a symbolic representation of all the empires that controlled the world from the time of the Egyptians to this present day. The fundamental controlling authority of those empires worked over the spheres of politics, economics, law, military, education, and to a great degree, religion.

Think of the power of the Egyptians, of Babylon, of Greece, and of Rome. Think of the British Empire and its navy, its commercial life, its state run religion, and its banking power. The False Prophet operates with *all* the power of the first Beast; *all* the authority and power, *all* the spheres and dimensions of an empire.

Think of the power he wields. How would it be to have ALL POWER over the western world's political, economic, legal, military, educational and religious areas of life?

The important point to be made here in no uncertain terms is that this is not just some religious entity moving with a new religious order of some sort. The false Prophet's power extends far beyond the sphere of the religious dimension. This thing moves with *ALL* authoritative power.

He Is Contemporary

And he exercises all the authority of the first beast *in his presence.*

Revelation 13:12
(emphasis mine)

The phrase, "in his presence" shows us that the two entities appear together, and that the power of the False Prophet is not delegated from the first Beast. It seems as though both of the two entities have the same authoritative power. The first Beast is apathetic towards the authority of the False Prophet. He doesn't seem to be intimidated by the power of the False Prophet. The reason for this is because the last phase of the construction of the Beast system with its ten horns is contingent on the False Prophet's success in pulling it all together.

We shall see in a moment the operation of the False Prophet's comprehensive authority. These facts are important because they help us acquire a greater objectivity about just who and what the False Prophet is.

To recapitulate the facts of the False Prophet:

1. The second Beast is a two-horned system, or two nation confederacy.

2. He will function during a period when the seventh head of the first Beast is healed from a fatal wound of war (a great sword). He is contemporary with the first Beast's last phase of completion.

3. He will have *all* the power of the first Beast.

The False Prophet also does great signs:

1. He will have power to call fire down from heaven.

2. He will be able to deceive the whole world, particularly through an image.

3. He will abolish all economic systems where cash is used as the medium of exchange and introduce a cashless system that will operate through 666 (Revelation 13:12-18).

The great signs that the second Beast performs will be dealt with in later chapters in more detail, but all these abilities and factors are at his disposal to construct the ten nations and the New World Order.

It is a great mistake to assign to the False Prophet the small task of merely building a new world religion. As can be seen, his power extends far beyond that.

When Shall These Things Be?

Today many believe that these manifestations of the second Beast will occur at some point in the future. The question must be asked, Are these abilities of the second Beast to be exercised in the future? Are they already in evidence?

The discussion of this topic will cause great pain to many people, because it calls into question one's pre-suppositional position on biblical prophecy (eschatology-the study of last things), and therefore their approach to the book of Revelation.

Looking At Revelation

Basically there are four possible ways of interpreting the book of Revelation:

1. The spiritual scheme--the Apocalypse is given to teach fundamental spiritual principles.

2. The preterist scheme--the book only teaches events taking place on earth during the Roman era, during the time of the apostle John's lifetime.

3. The historic scheme--the symbols in Revelation relate to events in the history of the world which are relevant to the welfare of the church from the first century to modern times.

4. The furturist scheme--insists that for the most part, the visions of the book will be future, toward the end of the age.

The question one has to ask oneself is, Which of the above positions is accurate? Which set of spectacles should be looked through?

There has been constant debate on this problem for hundreds of years, and the poor believer is left to ferret it out for himself. That each position has its merits is indisputable. In the North American church, by and large, the prominent view is the futurist scheme.

The futurist scheme, for the most part, insists that the visions of Revelation will be fulfilled toward the end of the age. While there may be a great deal of truth to this position, it also creates its own problem. The problem with futurism is this, the closer we move toward the end of the age, the more likely we are to overlook and miss the events predicted in the symbols, and assign their fulfillment to some future time. This view keeps pushing the fulfillment of events ahead into the future, so we never arrive.

This is not to say that history should conform to our conjectural whims because we are impatient for the fulfillment of prophecy, but the Lord told us clearly that, "You, brethren, are not in darkness, that the day should overtake you like a thief" (1 Thessalonians 5:4).

A careful study of history will show that the False Prophet has been with us for some time, and that he is alive and in the world today.

Chapter Nineteen

HISTORY OF THE FALSE PROPHET - THE NEW ZION

I t began with most of them as an escape from Feudalism and the despotism that reigned over their religious lives. England and Europe were basically without a middle class. The average person had no hope of ever holding land. All property was considered owned by the king, and was controlled by the very rich. The rest of the people were serfs. [1]

This was the system called Feudalism. In England the reigning king also dictated the nature of worship to God. Christianity was tightly controlled by the sovereign. [2]

Those in England that continued to dream dreams of freedom deeply desired a fresh start. They were willing to seek out and to brave the difficulties and harshness of the journey to the new world. The ones that ventured believed they were coming to the New Jerusalem, the promised land. The escape from England was looked at as an exodus from an Egypt, but they also viewed their awaited liberties in the new land with a prophetic sense of purpose. [3]

A Fresh Start

These visionaries had first hand knowledge of the terrible bondage of feudalism and despotism. They saw in America the potential fulfillment of all their hopes and dreams; a new nation based upon the Judeo-Christian law and morality of the sacred Scriptures. In the beginning there was a terrible price to be paid as they carved out a niche in the hostile world, but it was a small price as they considered the great opportunity which was in their hands and the potential that was before them. [4]

The Exodus

It started out as resistance to the Anglican Church. Religious oppression under the state run church eventually became so intolerable that those who had deep-seated convictions about God had to leave. They were the Separatists, and they moved to the mainland of Europe, to a place of refuge in Holland. After spending eleven years in exile from England, the hearts of the zealots still longed for a new freedom. The exhausting toil of eighteen hour workdays for meager wages was straining their sensibilities. Why not break free and move to the New World in America? [5]

Being a devout and religious people, they took council through corporate prayer. They believed that their God was inspiring them to brave the elements and trust Him for a new beginning in a far away land. [6] About a hundred of them crowded into the Mayflower, a ship roughly the size of a volleyball court, and for sixty-six days braved the awesome power of the mighty Atlantic Ocean. [7]

One year after landing at Plymouth Rock, almost half of the valiant band had starved to death. The Thanksgiving celebration later that year, however, was the beginning of an American tradition marking the rewards of their heroic faith in God. [8]

The Lords of England, on the other hand, and the other side of the Atlantic Ocean, viewed the colonists as rebels. Like Pharaoh of Egypt, they would not let the people go to the land of promise uncontested. Elitist elements within Britain sought to retain control and subdue the colonies. The new land, it was reasoned, must be kept under British control. [9]

The Bank of England

In 1692 Massachusetts opened a mint and began to issue coins, and later, its own paper notes. These notes were considered full legal tender. The notes could be borrowed at low interest rates by the citizens for all sorts of needs; business, homes, etc. The revenues that came from these low interest loans were used for public purposes, and thus kept taxes down. This was all done without the consent of England. Other colonies followed their lead and enjoyed great prosperity. The colonies paid no interest to anyone. [10]

In England, however, King William III made a decision to give William Paterson and associates a charter to establish a private bank. It was called the Bank of England. [11]

The King needed money to finance his war with France. This favor was extended in exchange for the loan. The bank had the exclusive privilege of issuing paper money and lending it at interest. With control of London and England's monetary system in hand, the bankers fixed their gaze on the New World, intensely motivated and determined to control its currency as well. [12]

By 1720 every colonial governor was instructed to stop issuing their own paper notes. The bankers in England slyly used the British Board of trade as their front, thus effecting decisions and manipulating the Parliament so that the English government would back their movements against the American colonies. The colonies refused to submit. The conflict that later boiled over in the American Revolution was under way, but the seed of that armed conflict was the control of money. [13]

During 1767, Ben Franklin tried to fiscally conciliate the colonies with the Crown Empire, but Franklin's diplomacy did not work. While Franklin was in England, former Prime Minister Granville spoke these words in the House of Commons. They became the guidance system for international banking.

I will tell the honorable gentlemen of a revenue that will produce something valuable in America. Make paper money for the colonies [under British control], issue it upon loan there, take the interest and apply it as you think proper. [14]

Because the English government held this underhanded vision it backed the Bank of England to the hilt. Therefore, the bank was ready to apply and enforce their policy of monetary control over the American colonies.

It should be clear that the intent of this policy was to enslave the New World in and through debt. The colonies refused this fiscal tyranny and met on June 10, 1775. There they resolved to create $2,000,000 in bills of credit that the united colonies would honor. This action was viewed by the British as open defiance and rebellion. The boiling point had been reached. In America the eruption that blasted forth came to be known as the Boston Tea Party. This was the event that launched the Revolutionary War. The momentum for the war, however, had begun building some 80 years earlier. [15]

The Boston Tea Party

The Boston Tea Party and the American Revolution expressed the deeply entrenched sentiments of those who yearned to be free from the overlordship of the British Empire. What the patriots were saying as they dumped the tea into Boston Harbor was that they were fed up with being taxed and having no control of their own credit or the printing of their own nation's money. [16]

The Americans, through taxation, were paying to be policed by a power they didn't want ruling over them. This was the initial reason for their exodus from Britain. The British had cunningly extorted from the colonies money which they used to garrison troops on American soil. They did this to maintain a watchful eye on the colonies. The war for independence was over a whole lot more than a little tax on tea.

Although the escape to the New World was to a great extent a religious matter, the Revolutionary war was fought over taxation, and more importantly, who would control capital in the new world, and how.

The Rothschilds

The Rothschilds, a family of Jewish lineage, were very shrewd in their dealings with money. They gained large sums by investment and later became bankers. Five sons of Rothschild dispersed throughout Europe and set up banking houses in strategic locations in different countries. [17]

About the turn of the century (1799) the Rothschilds, with increased financial power, allied themselves with the Masonic secret societies. Under cover of obscurity they successfully destabilized the European continent by financing the French Revolution from London, which became the seat of the Rothschilds' international banking dynasty. [18]

The Rothschilds and other banking families were secretly establishing new power centers as the dynastic monarchies of Europe were disintegrating. The influence of the bankers was exerted on both businesses and governments. [19]

Fledgling America was an obstacle to the schemes for British world control held by the monetary interests. The new nation continued to refuse the shackles of a central bank, and America's credit remained relatively free from foreign control. Because the lending power was not in the hands of the international manipulatiors they could not proceed with their global aspirations. [20]

The fundamental concept these pirates used in their business came from a promise in the Old Testament. "You will lend to many nations, but you will not borrow; and you will rule over many nations, but they will not rule over you." (Deuteronomy 15:6). The Rothschilds built on this principle, but subverted God's intent by lending at usurious rates. They believed that if they controlled the wealth of a nation, they could, by the power and influence of wealth, transcend the legal power of the state. They would often boast, "I care not who makes the laws of a nation, give me the wealth of a nation and I'll make the laws." [21] They conducted themselves along the lines of the blueprint for world control mapped out in the *Protocols of the Illuminati*. [22]

Adam Weishaupt—The Illuminati

Adam Weishaupt was a professor of considerable renown at Ingolstadt University. He was driven by an incredible, diabolical ambition to rule the world. Unlike others who sought the same prize, Weishaupt was not a crude gangster who could lead a band of thieves and rowdies. Neither was he a military type who sought conquest through sheer force. Weishaupt was an intellectual, a professor at law. His high-minded self conceit caused him to feel mentally superior to others. Received into the Masonic Order of his day, he found like minded comrades. [23]

Those who banded together with Weishaupt felt they were of such superior fiber that they should be running the world. A secret order was devised called the Illuminati, which would become the vehicle for world conquest. [24]

The Scope of the Illuminati

The Order of the Illuminati would embrace the entire world, to unite men from all places, all social classes and all religions, despite the diversity of their opinions and passions. The idea was to make them love this common interest, and bond to the point where, together or alone, they act as one individual. The ultimate objective was to bring happiness to the world. The philosophy behind this was the rather novel idea that the end--the happiness of the people--justified the means. [25]

The ultimate purposes of the Illuminati were to take over the world. Talent for the Order was screened by an elaborate system of initiation, as the initiate would have to pass from one degree to the next. Weishaupt carefully plotted each step of the way, making sure the weakest would not rise above the lowest levels of the Order. The bold, the ruthless and cynical were brought along to the highest levels of Reagent, Magus, and Rex. [26]

Illuminism and Free Masonry

Weishaupt believed that his organization needed a cover and a way to extend its power. In 1782 he successfully infiltrated the Masonic Order at the congress of Wilhelmsbad. [27]

In America, George Washington, who was a Mason, became aware of the movements of the Illuminati within the Masonic Order. A Christian minister gave Washington a book entitled *Proofs of A Conspiracy*. This was Washington's response to the book.

It was not my intention to doubt that the doctrines of
the Illuminati, and principles of Jacobinism, had not
spread to the United States. On the contrary, no one is
more fully satisfied of this fact than I am. The idea that
I meant to convey was that I did not believe the Lodges
of Freemasonry in this country had, as societies, endeavored to propagate the diabolical tenets of the
Illuminati. [28]

For the Order to gain its objective it was necessary to abolish
religion, governments, and private property. These the Order
deemed were the real obstacles to true happiness. This is exactly
what the communists have been advocating since 1848. But most
importantly, THE ILLUMINISTS AND LATER THE COMMU-
NISTS ADVOCATED THE CENTRALIZATION OF CREDIT IN
THE HANDS OF THE STATE BY MEANS OF A NATIONAL
BANK WITH STATE CAPITAL AND AN EXCLUSIVE MO-
NOPOLY. [29]

The Order of the Illuminati was driven underground in
Europe due to its plans being discovered, but the ideas, the plans,
and the goals have lived on in the Communist movement, the
ideas of John Ruskin, Cecil Rhodes, Rothschild, the Round Table,
and the C.F.R.

The British Spy System

The British never conceded that the American-declared
independence was to be accepted by them as the final inning in
British world hegemony. Their aims of world dominion would
not be frustrated by a few farmers and wild-eyed dreamers on the
other side of the earth.

In the late 18th century in the United States, two prominent
political figures squared off in a duel to the death. The battle is
remembered by most students of American history, but the
reasons for the hostilities between these two lay buried to this
day. The battle to the death involved Alexander Hamilton, the
father of the American banking system, and Aaron Burr, who at
one time was Vice-President of the United States. [30]

Exhuming the story reveals a mystery that provides a key in
unlocking important facts concerning Great Britain's continuous

struggle to regain control of America. America's economic development is directly related to Britain's attempts to seize this nation. Through this study it can be seen why today the citizens of this land are buried in mountainous debt, and thus monumental taxation. These are the same two issues that caused the American Revolution in the first place.

Since it was costly and difficult to maintain a war effort in the Western part of the world, especially with Europe in turmoil with the French Revolution in full swing, the British intelligence sent their spies into the United States with the intent of seizing the country from within. Their chief man of the hour was the Rothschild's agent, Aaron Burr. Burr was a fully trained agent of the Internationalists. Most importantly, Burr was a Scottish Rite Freemason of the 33rd degree. (The Illuminati infiltrated Scottish Rite Freemasonry). Here, in the person of Aaron Burr, can be seen the synthesis of the intent of the world bankers and the rationale of the Illuminati-infiltrated Scottish Rite Freemasonry. [31]

After becoming governor of New York, Burr helped obtain cheap loans for the Internationalists to buy up most of New York state. Burr helped found the Manhattan Bank (the Chase Manhattan Bank) and much has been written about his nefarious dealings in the South as he helped lay the groundwork for the Civil War in the first decade of the 1800s. [32]

When he sought to become President of the United States he was frustrated by Alexander Hamilton, who viewed him as a traitor. Burr was also highly suspected by George Washington, and history documents his family ties with Benedict Arnold, the most infamous traitor in American history. [33]

When he ran for President, Burr was narrowly defeated by Jefferson. Had it not been for Hamilton, Burr, the Rothschilds' agent, would have become President of the United States of America. So there is much behind the duel that most history books do not tell us, but the most important fact is yet to come.

The Bank of the U.S.A.

Alexander Hamilton is known today as the father of the American banking System. Even though Hamilton was a red-blooded American, he wanted a central bank (modeled after the French ideal). The French ideal was simply that certain prominent, successful, and intelligent men would control the affairs of the bank. Jefferson was against the charter of such a bank, fearing the issue of too much power in the hands of an elitist group. Even though these men be Americans, Jefferson felt it was too dangerous a proposition.

Burr also wanted a central bank, but his bank would have Internationalists as the ones in command. Burr killed Hamilton and fled the country to Britain. At issue again was who would control money in the New World, the British Banking system or an American group.

While Burr was Vice President, he and another Internationalist, Albert Gallatin (who had become Secretary of the Treasury) successfully sold the idea of the need for a balanced budget to Congress. By cutting military expenditures for the maintenance of the U.S. Navy, the defenses of the United States was weakened. This undermining of U.S. defenses opened the door for the British to stage another conflict. [34]

The second Revolutionary War (in 1812) was orchestrated by the Trojan Horse of the British spy system that had infiltrated American politics. The second Revolutionary War should have ended what Europeans called the American experiment. There is no explanation for America's survival except that it was an act of God, who personally intervened, thus saving the country. [35]

The Civil War - A Battle With the Bankers

By the time Abraham Lincoln became President, the United States had survived two Revolutionary Wars with Great Britain, and many hidden political intrigues, especially during Andrew Jackson's administration. The pesky child nation, America, was causing great delay to the global aspirations of the British Empire. After the failure to recharter the Bank of the United States, the European bankers began plotting the Civil War.

During Lincoln's administration, the British inspired the Civil War. The war would create the need, and the temptation to finance the war through borrowing. The plotters realized the American people would not accept a national bank without reason for having one. They decided upon a war. Wars are costly, and they force governments into a position where they must borrow to pay for them.

Who could the plotters induce to fight a war with America? Since America had become such a powerful nation, there was none to rival her in the Western Hemisphere.

The bankers made the decision to divide the nation into two parts, thereby creating an enemy for the United States. The overt issue for fighting was slavery, but the actual reason behind the Civil War was the splitting of the Union. The deeper motive was, of course, to seize control of the country by creating the financial need to borrow from the bankers at usurious interest rates, thus creating the need for a centralized bank. [36]

The whole story of the secession of the Southern States was given by George L. Bickley, who declared that he created the fateful war of 1861. He worked through an organization called the Knights of the Golden Circle, which engineered and spread secession. [37]

International Bankers Lending Control

The British bankers at that time also controlled the fledgling American banks, which offered to loan Abraham Lincoln money to fight the war. Lincoln wisely refused, and created the famous Lincoln greenbacks with which he financed the Civil War. [38]

Abraham Lincoln, in a famous address, declared:

> At what point, then, is the approach of danger to be expected? I answer, if it ever reach us it must spring up among us, it cannot come from abroad. If destruction be our lot, we must ourselves be its author and finisher. As a nation of free men we must live through all time or die of suicide. [39]

Lincoln's refusal to finance the union through debt to the Internationalists demonstrated his keen insight into their strategy for global dominion. Hence he financed the Civil War by printing the Lincoln greenbacks.

In both respects, with regard to the Civil War, and the British banker's attempt to seize control of the economics of America, once again the aims of the one-worlders were frustrated. America remained in control of her own credit. The result of this victory in maintaining control was low interest loans for entrepreneurs, which led to great business expansion. This great expansion in the post-Civil War era enhanced the fears of those who sought to bring the world into a One-World Order. If America was allowed to continue to expand then she would be a major, perhaps impossible, obstacle in the way of the goal.

America, for one hundred years, was able to avoid total control of her capital by the international bankers. Lincoln was most certainly a great irritant to the aspirations of the globalists, and was the last president to seek categorically a halting of the globalist drive toward a One-World Government. It cost him his life, as he was murdered by John Wilkes Booth, an agent of the Internationalists. [40]

When America emerged from the Civil War as a great industrial power, it was due to the effective centralization of capital and credit within the Federal Government, thanks to Lincoln. It was America's control over her own capital that was making America prosperous, but it was the aim of the international bankers to change all that.

Lincoln was the victim of a major conspiracy, a conspiracy so important that even the European bankers were involved. Lincoln had to be eliminated because he dared to oppose the attempt to force a central bank on the United states. He became an example to those who would later oppose such machinations in high places. Could it be that 100 years later J.F.K. was also a victim of this same intrigue?

Chapter Twenty

HISTORY OF THE FALSE PROPHET - THE POST CIVIL WAR ERA

It became crystal clear to the Globalists after the American Civil War that America had to be stopped. Frederick Engels, the British industrialist, was one of many who felt that the war would be the end to the American Republic. The victory of the North proved him wrong. Now the tremendous threat of the American system loomed an even greater shadow over the vast British Empire and continental Europe. A more vigorous strategy was plotted and pursued to finally overthrow America, England's now almost one hundred year old rebellious child.

A plan to counter the great expansion had to be conceived. A new economic warfare would be waged. The force of this overthrow centered on the nation's money and credit. This was done by contracting U.S. currency (which was the greenbacks) and lowering tariff barriers so that American markets could be exploited. Low tariffs meant that American industry would not be protected from foreign competition. This free trade policy was sought to exploit the markets of America, and to suck money away from circulation in the States. In other words, in the eyes of the British, the greenbacks had to go, because they kept the bankers from being in control.

Then the international pirates sought to bring about reform by replacing industry builders with foreign agents in seats of economic and political power. In order to conquer America, her financial sovereignty must, of necessity, come to an end. This became the sole front of the Internationalists' focus in their aspirations for a One-World Government. [1]

English Economic Counter-Attack

Conspirators went out to the U.S.A. to assail the greenbacks. The English-backed Golden Club was implanted in the Eastern United States for the sole purpose of throttling the successes of Lincoln's economic policies. After much wrangling and dissimulation, restrictions were placed upon the greenbacks. [2]

The bankers fought hard against the Government's attempt to recapture its own credit and money. They emerged from their war upon Lincoln's greenbacks with the prize. The restrictions that were placed upon the greenbacks caused a perception that made them inflationary. With clever manipulation the bankers were able to expand and contract the economy. They would not accept the greenbacks in payment for lands they had bought from the government. They demanded gold. For many years there was a general looting of the government's gold and the huge banking house of J.P. Morgan was built as an International Banking island upon the American soil. [3]

During the Administration of Abraham Lincoln, the powerful London-based banking house of Rothschild was behind the efforts to throttle the control of credit and money in America and to seize it. Rothschild wrote in a letter to Mr. Belmont warning ruin to those who might oppose the payment of U.S. Bonds in coin, or who might advocate their liquidation in greenbacks. [4]

The Internationalists refused to be defeated. Neither the Revolutionary War nor the second Revolutionary War, nor the failure of the rechartering of the bank, nor the failure of the Civil War would deter them. They never ceased working to subjugate and recapture America. However, a new strategy was planned. The British intelligence, under the control of the Internationalists sought to undermine the new nation from within.

Economic War & Political Intrigue
Frederick Engels

Frederick Engels was a brilliant British industrialist whose business depended greatly on cheap American slave cotton. This man, who was the most *famous* of all British industrialists, was one who paid great homage and respect to the East India-born think tank. The think tank mind trust included men like Thomas Carlyle, John Stuart Mill, Thomas Malthus and Charles Darwin, who had great influence on Engels. Their political-economic-socialist ideas, based upon feudalism, became Engels' launching pad for his development of the ideology of Communism. Frederick Engels was the founder of Marxist Communism and author of its doctrine. He was personal mentor of Karl Marx.

What was most greatly feared by the British Internationalists was beginning to truly threaten their plans for entire global control. America and her nation-building Republican system was being brought to the mainland of Europe by Germany. It was being accomplished by Frederick List, who had been sent to America to study the American System. [5]

List, after watching the success of the American Republican model, believed it was his duty and responsibility to promote everything which may increase the wealth and power of *the nation*. Tariffs must be erected to protect fledgling industry from nations that would attempt to loot by bringing cheaper goods. List saw the evil of free trade. [6]

The British Imperial System was the antithesis of this. Those in control knew the advantages of a free trade system and its power to maintain the expansion of its own economy and world sphere of control.

As the thrust of the American system's influence grew and had become introduced to Germany, a secret British offensive was launched against these neo-German Republicans and Abraham Lincoln's economic program in the United States.

It was in 1843 that Frederick Engels, father of communism, entered the fray. In his first treatise on economics, he attacked Christianity (the base of the American Republican system) and carefully directed his readers to the free trade versus protectionist battle then going on in Germany. He pointed out how essential it was to follow the position of free trade as the "Proper course of action" and "the shorter road to wealth." [7]

Engels, after winning over Karl Marx, published their first co-authored book, *The Condition of the Working Class* . The book served as a false-prophetic warning to the German working class of the horrors in store for them if (energized by America) imported industrialization developed. [8]

Marx then teed off on Frederick List, through his book, *The National System of Political Economy*, and branded List as a propagator of the special interests of German manufacturers.

The titanic battle between the ideologies of Republicanism and Feudalism stymied the industrialization and unification of Germany until the latter part of the 19th century. As the Engels/Marx communist duet was gaining the upper hand in slowing the growth of mainland European industrialization, they used the same fear inspired by these literary weapons for International Globalism, to undermine and seize the American Republic by destroying Abraham Lincoln's Republican economic reforms.

Lincoln's greenbacks mobilized national credit in America and thus financed the victory of the North in the Civil War. Had Lincoln surrendered to the temptation of the banker's loans (with exorbitant interest rates) truly the borrower (the U.S.A.) would have become slave to the lender (England). Lincoln saw the evils of free trade ideology, and the slavery system that supported cheap cotton imported by the British for their textile mills. This enabled the British to maintain a tremendous economic edge over the rest of the world. [9]

Britain in control of raw materials could bring the cotton to England, then sell it back in finished products at high profit not only in America, but all over the world. If ever these nations were to industrialize and manufacture their own finished products, they could erect trade barriers and destroy the monopoly that the English enjoyed over these worldwide markets.

Here the ideology of Communism and British Free Trade Expansionism was the strange, and not so strange, brew that was created to stifle the Christian-based Republicanism of America and the advancement of industrialization to the European continent, which could enable nations to break out of feudalist indentured slavery. [10]

The Communist movement was one of a number of weapons created by British strategists to counter the spread of the American system of political ideas and nationalist economic organization to the European continent.

Britain's Conquest of Mammon
The Rothschild's War-Chest for Globalism

In the late 19th century and into the 20th, with the American purse falling more and more into the hands of the International Banking Elite, the final conflict to set up the 100 year old Illuminist's dream of an American central bank was staged.

As the Internationalists orchestrated the depression of 1907, the American populace was finally psychologically prepared to receive a *centralized banking plan*. A plan that promised to control and stabilize the flow of capital. It would be a central bank that promised to be run by the government. It would be a bank that promised to see that there would never again be a shortage of money in circulation, and thus always be able to keep the life blood of the economy moving. [11]

Great Deception

The International planners knew, OH! how they knew, that the American people would never accept a plan that enabled private interests to control the bank. The American people wanted a bank that was controlled by the government, not by private banking houses like the Rothschilds and J.P. Morgans.

> I care not who makes the laws of the nations. Give me the wealth of the nations and I'll make the laws.
> Rothschild [12]

Under cloak of great, great secrecy the plotters of world financial control and global world government retreated to a place called...*Jekyll Island*. There they plotted and schemed and created with great subtlety the Federal Reserve Act. The

Rothschilds sent their special agent, Paul Warburg, to head up the delegation. His mission was to stage the takeover of the American banking system.

Jekyll Island

Warburg called together the most powerful money families in America. Then, with their support he drafted two infamous plans that laid the groundwork for the seizure of the American banking system. Actually there was one plan with two different names. At Jekyll Island, the representatives of these powerful families planned and made agreements that framed the diabolical plot. Plan 1 was called the Aldrich Plan. Plan 2 was called the Federal Reserve Act. History records which one of these identical plans was accepted by the U.S. Congress. [13]

The Federal Reserve

The Federal Reserve Act created what has become today the central bank of the United States of America, or the Federal Reserve System.

Contrary to popular understanding, the Fed is *not* controlled by the U.S. Government, but by representatives who are selected by the International Bankers themselves. [14] The Fed's decision-making processes remind one of the fox who guarded the chicken house. Unbeknownst to the American public the Federal Reserve System is a private corporation which in 1913, by craft and guile, became the American banking system. Actually, it has been given this name for deceptive purposes. [15]

George Washington, the Father of his country, spoke these words of wisdom concerning the formation of a central bank.

Shall a few designing men, for their own aggrandizement, and to glorify their own avarice, overset the goodly fabric we have been rearing at the expense of much time, blood and treasure? [16]

Papa George saw the evil desire of the International Bankers and what they sought to accomplish with a central bank. As a result of Washington's statement, when the founding fathers met at the Constitutional Convention they assigned to the Congress the control of finances by these words:

> Congress shall have the power to coin money and regulate the value thereof. [17]

The purpose of this delegation of authority to the Congress was to specifically prevent robbery and exploitation by a select few. The Federal Reserve Act of December 23, 1913 (With Woodrow Wilson refusing to veto the passage of the bill by Congress) took away from the powers of Congress, and thus the American people, the power to coin or print money, and gave it to a private printing company called the Federal Reserve. Basically, what this meant was that the Fed could print money and charge interest. The revenues derived from that interest would accrue to the personal benefit of the principal stock holders of the Federal Reserve (Corporation) System.

This is exactly what Thomas Jefferson feared, what Abraham Lincoln expressed, and what George Washington warned of. Victory in the very issue for which the founding patriots gave their lives during the Revolutionary war had now been handed over to those they so valiantly fought against.

The Federal Reserve Act was passed on December 23, 1913 while most of the Congress was home for Christmas. But what did the plan allow for? The very thing Aaron Burr sought 100 years earlier, a central bank in the United states controlled by the International Bankers from London.

The purpose of the long sought after establishment and control of that system was the age old motive of the subjugation of the American colonies by the British as has been previously stated. The seizure of the money making privilege, and the control of credit by the bank, guaranteed the necessary power to establish the funding instrument for an inevitable Global World Government. The ability to expand and contract credit was now securely in the hands of the Internationalists. Now they had the ability to centralize and concentrate capital into the hands of an elite group that could control the world.

The sinister brilliance of the Fed has, over the last eighty years, looted the American people and created the enormous national debt. The ability for it to create fiat money (money that is not backed by silver or gold) by simply making a notation in a ledger, has not only created great inflationary forces, but also initially led to the creation of the graduated income tax.

The Internationalists also possess controlling interests in munitions companies, and reap huge profits from war. Governments must buy from them to fight the wars the Internationalists create. Those borrowing nations must then promise to pay back the capital for their war machine by issuing promissory notes called bonds. The greatest borrower of these funds is America. The combined debt of the world does not equal the amount of borrowed capital that America owes.

The government can make these pledges (bonds) of repayment to the Fed because the people of the U.S.A. yearly pay their taxes (graduated taxes) which guarantee repayment. These massive yearly revenues have come under the control of the Fed.

The Conquest of America

When America finally lost control of her money she gave up financial freedom. Today money is expensive. When borrowing takes place today, the interest rates are so high that those seeking to own homes pay three times their mortgages by the time the loan is paid off. Home mortgages are just the tip of the iceberg.

It can be said that when America lost control of her money she was ostensibly recaptured by Britain, or more specifically, by those who control Britain. Very slowly, almost without perception, America has become, and is becoming, a socialized nation. The manipulation of our monetary system by the creation of debt, and the necessity for high taxes, is creating a situation where more and more freedom is being lost. This phenomenon is forcing out a middle class and creating a neo-feudalism. The average American doesn't realize he has become captured by the very dragon his forefathers escaped some 200 years ago. The Bible says, "Who is able to wage war with [the beast]?" (Revelation 13:4).

Although America began as a nation under God, with the Bible as the foundation for the United States Constitution, the seizure of this once great and free nation actually has taken place without the knowledge of the populace.

Chapter Twenty One

HISTORY OF THE FALSE PROPHET - ANGLO-AMERICANISM

A global world government in the modern era should not be viewed as a 19th century idea. The powerful forces of the Illuminati that unleashed the French Revolution in 1789 clearly show that a New World Order had been in the making since the 18th century. [1]

Throughout the 1800s in the United States the idea of Globalism was maintained by forces within the British Empire. Three prominent men in the latter part of the century who kept the dream moving forward were John Ruskin, Cecil Rhodes, and Alfred Milner. Their desire was to unite the English speaking people of the world and to create a global commonwealth of nations patterned after the ideals of the British Empire, but controlled by English speaking people of the aristocracy for the good of the world. [2]

John Ruskin-Rhodes-Milner
The Round Table

John Ruskin, mentor of both Cecil Rhodes and Alfred Milner (father of the Round Table), was an ardent student of Plato's *Republic*, the same well from which Karl Marx drank.

Ruskin believed that the state should take control of the means of all production and distribution, and organize them for the good of the people. "My continual aim has been to show the eternal superiority of some men to others, sometimes even of one man to all others," Ruskin taught that the ruling class of England had a world mission. [3]

The World Mission

Ruskin taught the students of Oxford University that they were the next leaders of the mission, that they were the ones who would carry on the tradition, that they were the possessors of a magnificent tradition of education, rule of law, beauty, freedom, decency, and self discipline, but this tradition could not be saved unless it was extended to the lower classes of England, and to the non-English masses of the world. If these two classes were not reached, the upper-class Englishmen would ultimately be submerged by these majorities, and the tradition would be lost. [4]

Cecil Rhodes

Cecil Rhodes was one student in attendance that day and he caught the vision. With support from Lord Rothschild he launched a lifetime of concerted effort to Federate the World. [5] His ambitious goals included:

1. The extension of the British rule throughout the world
2. Perfecting a plan of emigration from the United Kingdom for colonization by British subjects of all lands where the means of livelihood are attainable by energy, labor, and enterprise

3. THE ULTIMATE RECOVERY OF THE UNITED STATES OF AMERICA AS AN INTEGRAL PART OF THE BRITISH EMPIRE

4. The consolidation of the whole Empire

5. A system of colonial representation in the Imperial Parliament which may tend to weld together the disjointed members of the Empire

6. The foundation of so great a power as to hereafter render wars impossible and promote the best interests of humanity

All this he endeavored to do without mention of material reward, an idea fashioned after the religious brotherhood of the Jesuits, "a church for the extension of the British Empire." [6]

The ideas of these men, advanced by the backing of Anglo-American banking houses, created secret societies, which in turn made secret agreements between England and the United States. These secret treaties brought the two countries together into an Anglo-American alliance with the secret goal of a New World Order. In England the secret society, which operated in London, was called the Round Table. [7]

The League of Nations

When the planned seizure of the United States economy finally occurred in 1913, the formation of the two-horned Beast (the world capital conglomerate) was complete. The object of the conquest of mammon (the god of this world) was to enable the concentration of financial power in the hands of an elite. What they needed now was a new world political system to manage the aspirations of the British dreamers.

The first attempt at a new world order was the League of Nations. It came at the culmination of World War I. The general idea of the League of Nations started during the war with a group of allied statesmen, notably British and American.[8] Winston Churchill supports this view.

> The League of Nations was an Anglo-Saxon conception arising from the moral earnestness of persons of similar temperament on both sides of the Atlantic. [9]

The League Fails!

The League of Nations, which was put forward by the American President, Woodrow Wilson, failed to gain entire acceptance. Paradoxically, though the rest of the world accepted the idea of the League of Nations, factions within the United States resisted the plan. The plan to create a League of Nations failed.

The Council on Foreign Relations

Other powerful men that were disciples of Ruskin joined their lives and fortunes with Rhodes and later formed the Round Table. Alfred Milner became the chief trustee after Rhodes' death. Round Table groups were established in other protectorates and the United States. In 1919-27 the U.S. group became known as the Council of Foreign Relations, or the C.F.R. [10]

The story of how the secret society of Rhodes-Milner axis extended its influence to the United States is supplied by Dr. Carroll Quigley:

> The American branch of this organization, called at times the Eastern Establishment, has played a very significant role in the history of the United States. . . . Since 1925 there have been substantial contributions from wealthy individuals and from foundations, and firms associated with the International Banking Fraternity, especially the Carnegie United Kingdom Trust, and other organizations associated with J.P. Morgan, the Rockefeller and Whitney families, and the associates of Lazard Brothers and of Morgan, Granfell, and Company. [11]

The C.F.R. today has over two thousand members who represent the elite in government, labor, business, finance, communications and the academy. The primary reason the C.F.R. remains virtually unknown to the American people is because of Article II of the C.F.R. by-laws. This article requires that the meetings of the membership remain secret, and anyone releasing the contents of these meetings is subject to instant dismissal. [12]

The Motivation for the C.F.R.

The intellectuals who founded the C.F.R. felt there was a need for a world government, but that the American people were not ready for it. After the League of Nations treaty failed to pass the Senate, the C.F.R. was founded specifically to condition the people to accept a world government as being a desirable solution to the world's problems. [13]

Many of the founders had been involved in the negotiations leading to the Treaty of Versailles after World War I, including: Col. Edward Mandell House (who was secretly involved in the selection of Woodrow Wilson, and operated behind the scenes as a secret Secretary of State), Walter Lippmann (later to become one of the Liberal Establishment's favorite syndicated columnists), John Foster Dulles (later to become President Eisenhower's Secretary of State), Allen Dulles (later to become the director of the Central Intelligence Agency) and Christian Herter (later to become Dulles' successor as Secretary of State). [14]

Financiers of the C.F.R.

The original money behind the C.F.R. came from J.P. Morgan, John D. Rockefeller, Bernard Baruch, Paul Warburg, Otto Kahn, and Jacob Schift, among others. Two of those named above were present at Jekyll Island for the drafting of the Federal Reserve Act. Two of the most outstanding names were J. P. Morgan and Paul Warburg, who through Kuen Loeb and Co. represented the Rothschilds of England. [15]

On November 25, 1959, in an issue of its own publication,, *Foreign Affairs*, Study No. 7, the C.F.R. detailed its own exact purpose as:

> Advocating the building of a *new international order* which may be responsible to world aspirations for peace, and for social and economic change...an international order...including states labelling themselves as Socialist [Communist].

The words New International Order are catch words for a New World Government. [16]

This is what former Rear Admiral Chester Ward (USN, Ret.), told the American people about the intention of the C.F.R.. Ward was a former member of the C.F.R..

> The power clique in these elitist groups have on objective in common; they want to bring about the surrender of the sovereignty and national independence of the United States.
> A second clique of international members in the C.F.R. comprise the Wall Street International Bankers, and their key agents. They want the world banking monopoly from whatever power ends up in control of global government. They would probably prefer that this be an all powerful United Nations Organization, but they are also prepared to deal with a One World Government controlled by the Soviet Communists if the U.S. sovereignty is ever surrendered to them. [17]

Ward went on to say that their overall influence is used in promoting disarmament and submergence of U.S. sovereignty and national independence into an all-powerful One-World Government.

Membership in the C.F.R. reads like a veritable *Who's Who in American Politics*. Forty-seven attendees of the American delegation to the founding of the U.N. were C.F.R. members. Twelve of the last eighteen Secretaries of Treasury were C.F.R. members. Another twelve of the last sixteen Secretaries of State have been C.F.R. members. The Department of Defense, created in 1947 has had fifteen Secretaries, nine of which have been C.F.R. members. Every Allied commander in Europe and every U.S. ambassador to N.A.T.O. has been a member of the C.F.R. [18]

Since the inception of the C.F.R., almost every President elected has been a member. Although Ronald Reagan was not a member, his key appointees were. [19]

The C.F.R. and the Round Table form the hidden governments of the United States and Great Britain. They have been forged together for the purpose of bringing about the dream of Ruskin and Forbes, which is a New World Order. [20]

Chapter Twenty Two

THE TWO HORNED BEAST

I t should be no secret at this point that the two horns of the second beast are the two alleged Christian nations, Great Britain and the United States of America.

These two nations, through secret Anglo-American alliances, which began in the late 1800s, were brought together and are moving the whole world into a Global World Government, or New World Order. [1] It is the function of the two-horned beast to serve the interests of the ten-horned beast. "And he makes the earth and those who dwell in it to worship the first beast." (Revelation 13:12). It is this second Beast that works to construct the last phase of the first Beast.

These two horns, or kingdoms, were taken over by the International Money Powers seated in London. To Western observers, the U.S.A. looks Christian from the outside, but underneath there is a *hidden government* . "He had two horns like a lamb, and he spoke as a dragon," (Revelation 13:11). The same holds true for England. This Protestant nation, is in reality controlled by the hidden government and money powers there.

The inability to see this as a fulfillment of biblical prophecy is due to the lack of a clear perception of European history, and egocentricity on the part of Western theologians that have continually been blinded by the dualism of their dispensational theology and a naivete that arises from a *Yankee Doodle* Gospel. It is a sad fact that America has become an instrument of unrighteousness in the hands of *the god of this world*. The failure to perceive this truth perpetuates the situation.

The Bankers' Money Machine
Wars and Rumors of Wars

It is through the creation of "wars and rumors of wars," (Matthew 24:6) that the Internationalists have been able to create the condition that would warrant a global socialistic state. They have flooded the world with red ink and have brought the world into economic bondage through debt usury, thereby enslaving the people of the world. How do wars and rumors of wars create debt and thus usury?

When the Federal Reserve Bank was created in 1913, it effectively mobilized the credit of the United States of America. What this meant was the Fed, along with the European Banking system, had the necessary resources in hand to lend to the nations on a new and unprecedented scale. With this new tool in hand (the labor of the United States guaranteeing the potential loans to the world) the Internationalists could swamp the world in debt.

How? By creating wars so that nations must borrow to build their war machinery. It takes billons to build great warships, planes and weapons for warfare. Imagine if one could be the bank that could underwrite the loans to the nations who were energized to go to war. With that kind of clout one might be tempted to create a war just to make tremendous sums off the interest from the loans to those nations. One could even back both sides and not care who won the war since interest income would be made from both sides. Then, after the war ended, nations would have to rebuild their infrastructure; loans would be made to rebuild the houses, the factories, the businesses. With this money-making strategy one could gain absolute economic power over the entire earth.

It is an interesting coincidence that World War I began in 1914, just after the Internationalists established control of the American banking system and the mobilization of American credit (December 23, 1913). The beginning of the hostilities that plunged the whole world into war are unclear to this day. Could it have been the International Bankers that started the war to end all wars?

Through intrigue, through stealth, through manipulation of the nations, this has been the plan of the elite International Bankers; seizure of the earth through the creation of enormous debt. The magnitude of the global debt is staggering. The United States has been totally seized and enslaved. The debt of the United States is greater than the total debt of the entire world. [2]

The Cold War

In the Western world (especially North America) the apparent collapse of communism in eastern Europe has been lauded as Democracy's triumph, a tribute to the success of the free enterprise system. What has not been perceived, however, is that communism has produced the first stages of a global socialism. It has literally come about by communism serving as a counterweight to capitalism. The cold war between East and West that was created resulted in huge military expenditures for both sides to maintain the balance of power.

The need for both parties to maintain military equilibrium created the necessity for enormous amounts of capital. The bankers stood ready to loan. Once again the use of the bankers' insidious banking machine of wars and rumors of wars has further mired the world in debt, and advanced their own economic grasp and control of the planet.

Since communism has been a chief ingredient of the bankers scheme in this decade, let's back up and trace its roots.

Communism

That communism is an English invention is not a new idea. The articulation of communism was put forward by Karl Marx, whose mentor was British industrialist Frederick Engels. Their primary reason for the expounding of this politico-economic ideology was to thwart the advance of democracy in the nation building principles expressed in the Monroe Doctrine (which was based upon George Washington's advice of avoiding entanglements with Europe). These principles were beginning to be imported into Germany, and they posed a tremendous threat to British economic supremacy. The Industrial Revolution that came to the British Isles brought astounding revenues into the coffers of the Bank of England and the Empire itself. [3]

The controllers of Britain were fearful of potential competition on the world scene. They didn't want the rest of the world to industrialize and compete with British goods and markets. Thus came the *Communist Manifesto* and *Das Capital*, whose fundamentals at the time espoused international free trade which, of course, was a contradiction of the Monroe Doctrine's ideology of protectionism.

Internationalism was of tremendous advantage to the British since they already had control of world markets, and a terrible disadvantage to the rest of the world, whose economies were already exploited by the British.

Communism was invented by British subjects, but its basic elements were taken from Illuminism. The basic strategy of Communism was to stage economic war with continental Europe and the United States. The objective was the maintenance and control of world markets. The actual roots of communism go back to Adam Weishaupt. [4]

The New World Order in the 20th Century

Later in the 20th century, when the idea of globalism had matured, the front for the breakout of the New World Order was exported to Russia in the Bolshevik Revolution. [5] The Czar would not borrow from the Western Banks, which would have enslaved Russia through debt usury. He had to be overthrown.

The ideology of world communism (having been established through the Internationalist financed Bolshevik Revolution of 1917) established the necessary counter balance weighted against democracy/capitalism. Since World War II the two have become melded into an emerging global socialistic state.

The initial funding for the revolution came from a Rothschild controlled banking house in the United States called Kuen Loeb Co. [6] The leadership and intelligence of the movement was supplied by various Marxists who lived in New York. Some were Jews who *had repudiated* their ancient *Hebraic* ancestry. Many were not Jews, but all, like Karl Marx, had a fanatical political zeal to build a nation state that would encompass the whole world, a global masonry. Although the primitive breakout of this ideology can be traced to the French Revolution in 1789, the Bolshevik Revolution further advanced what is yet to come, which is a "World Government seated in Jerusalem of Zion." [7]

With the Revolution, the Russian state struggled to keep on its feet, and had it not been for the propping up of the Russian economy by the West, there would have been total failure of that regime during the 20s and 30s.

When WWII came to an end, the allies allowed the war to drag on for another unnecessary two years just to allow the Russians to come down and seize Eastern Europe. A window of truth that supports this allegation can be seen when General Patton had marched through Italy, but then was mysteriously re-routed through France. Why was he not allowed to invade Germany and end the war? He was willing, ready, and able to take his troops into Berlin.

This military faux pas has never been understood by the world, but the truth is that the Russians needed time to come down into Eastern Europe. The bankers needed their antithesis. The politicians followed orders. General Patton was too good at being a soldier and military man. He was messing up the predetermined plan of the plotting bankers.

These strategic political decisions were made to enable communism to serve as the great antithesis to capitalism and lead the way for the inevitable synthesis of capitalism and communism into global socialism that has begun to emerge at the beginning of the nineties.

The successful affect of the antithesis (U.S.S.R.) upon the West, when one lives in the West, is difficult to discern. The Mega-international corporations owned by the International Elite have created the tyranny of centralized capital, and the increasing disappearance of the American entrepreneur. Quickly freedom is being lost, and the ability to compete against the enormity of centralized capital is almost impossible. The tremendous debt created by the necessary military defense of America from the antithesis (Russia) has enslaved the West.

The Coming Trouble

While it took two world wars, the Balfour Declaration, and the holocaust to set up the state of Israel, or Zion, it is not the fulfillment of biblical prophecy as most Christians believe.

> Then it will happen on that day that the Lord will again recover the second time with His hand the remnant of His people,...and will assemble the banished ones of Israel, and will gather the dispersed of Judah from the four corners of the earth.
>
> Isaiah 11:11, 12

It is this particular Scripture that is cited by Christians as the fulfillment of prophecies for the Jews current return to Zion. But under close scrutiny, this promised second return of the Jews to the land will occur during the Millennial Kingdom.

This Scripture, read in context shows that the Bible says:

> And the wolf will dwell with the lamb, and the leopard will lie down with the kid, and the calf and the young lion and the fatling together; and a little boy will lead them. Also the cow and the bear will graze; their young will lie down together; and the lion will eat straw like the ox. And the nursing child will play by the hole of the cobra, and the weaned child will put his hand on the viper's den.
>
> Isaiah 11:6-8

The Real New Age

The time period of this occurrence has yet to come. These traits of animal behavior are unique and have never occurred. The time period spoken of comes when the whole world is renewed by God during the Millennial reign of Jesus Christ on earth.

It is during the Millennial reign that the curse upon the earth is lifted and these interesting changes in the animal kingdom occur. When that day comes in the not too distant future, then God signals for the ancient Jews to return to Israel.

If the return of the Jews according to biblical prophecy is yet in the future, then what has the world been witnessing since the turn of the century with the Zionist movement, and the birth of the State of Israel in 1948?

The Great Snare

The answer to this question is both deep and prophetic. What we are witnessing in the Middle East and Israel today is the set up of *the great snare*. David says: "May their table before them become a snare; and when they are in peace, may it become a trap." (Psalms 69:22)

Jesus also explained that this trap is one that will come over all the earth.

> Be on guard, that your hearts may not be weighted down with dissipation and drunkenness and the worries of life, and that day come on you like a trap; for it will come upon *all those who dwell on the face of all the earth.*
>
> Luke 21:34, 35
> (emphasis mine)

The events that are taking place today are all leading to the fulfillment of these Scriptures, the snare to the Jews and a trap to the whole world. It is the orchestration of these world-wide events that will lead to the fulfillment of the great weeks prophecy in Daniel 9:24-27.

While time and space do not permit a careful scrutiny of the whole of this text, it is important to restate the basics for those that have never taken a hard look at this portion of Scripture.

Chapter Twenty Three

DANIEL'S SEVENTY WEEKS

Seventy weeks have been decreed for your people and your holy city, to finish the transgression, to make an end of sin, to make atonement for iniquity, to bring in everlasting righteousness, to seal up vision and prophecy, and to anoint the most holy place.

So you are to know and discern that from the issuing of a decree to restore and rebuild Jerusalem until Messiah the Prince there will be seven weeks and sixty-two weeks; it will be built again, with plaza and moat, even in times of distress.

Then after the sixty-two weeks the Messiah will be cut off and have nothing, and the people of the prince who is to come will destroy the city and the sanctuary. And

> its end will come with a flood; even to the end there
> will be war; desolations are determined.
>
> Daniel 9:24-26

This prophecy is the famous weeks prophecy that clearly shows forth the first advent of the Messiah as being 69 weeks from the going forth of a decree. The 69 weeks means 69 units of seven, or 69 weeks of years. Sixty-nine weeks or 69 sevens equates to 483 years (69 x 7 = 483).

From the time the King of Persia (King Artaxerxes) issued a decree (445 B.C.) exactly 483 years elapsed until Jesus was crucified, or was cut off. The crucifixion occurred around 30 A.D.

The prophecy begins, however, with Daniel being told that there will be 70 weeks decreed upon his people. The initial decree dealt with a 70 week period, and the second decree with a 69 week period encompassed by the initial 70 weeks. Initially 70 weeks of years (7 x 70 = 490) were determined, but according to the rest of the Scripture, only 483 years transpired. What happened to the last seven years? Seven years are still to be fulfilled in the future. The 69 weeks of years ended at the crucifixion and the last seven years of the fist decree have yet to happen.

> And he will make a firm covenant with the many for
> one week, but in the middle of the week he will put
> a stop to sacrifice and grain offering; and on the
> wing of abominations will come one who makes
> desolate, even until a complete destruction, one
> that is decreed, is poured out on the one who makes
> desolate.
>
> Daniel 9:27

Here is the last seven years in the 27th verse. The *he* that is referred to in the 27th verse is not Jesus Christ, but rather the prince of the people that destroy the city of Jerusalem. This prince arrives on the scene to make a covenant with the many during the last seven years, or last week of the 70 weeks.

This Scripture sums up the advent for the timing of the Anti-christ. The Anti-christ will years of this famous decree. He will make a covenant with the many for seven years.

All the political manipulations and maneuvering that we are witnessing today is the set up for this world ruler and dictator. It is the trap that is coming on the world which Christ himself predicted in Luke 21:34, 35. It was also foretold by King David of the Jews. We are rapidly approaching the time when a man will step forth and cut a world-wide covenant with the many.

This is exactly what is before us now in the peace talks of the Middle East. While the people of the world truly hate war, there must be great care in not accepting the *PEACE MOVEMENT.*

Any guarantee of world-wide peace, or perhaps the world ecological movement, must be watched as the coming covenant with the many. Since the world is near economic collapse with the tremendous world-wide indebtedness, it is possible that the covenant with the many could include an economic agreement. It may be a combination of all three.

Since the WEEKS prophecy is to last for 490 years, there will be a seven year conclusion to purge the Jews, God's people, and to prepare them for the end, then the Millennium of Messiah.

Though this is called a snare and a trap, it will be the means to complete the necessary work of faith in the Jews, and bring in the Millennial Kingdom. Thus the nation of Israel has been gathered for judgement, and not for a blessing.

The orchestration of events that has brought about a return of this remnant has been by the hands of those who have seized control of the reins of international capital. Through political intrigue and the force and power of mammon (the riches of the world) they have seated the Jews in their homeland. God allowed this to take place. The nation of Israel, as well as the whole world, will be deceived by this prince (Anti-christ) who will come during this last week (seven years) of Daniel's prophecy.

God has allowed this to happen with capital controlled by the international world bankers, constructing a global totalitarian socialistic state, with the city of Jerusalem eventually to be the seat of World Government. *The United States' seized economy and the British banking system are the focal points of the war chest for this behemoth undertaking.*

Now as we enter the final hours before the Anti-christ comes, the formation of the ten horns of the Beast, or the amalgamation of the European continent has surfaced. The resolution for a unified Germany should come as no surprise as it represents the final healing of the fatal wound of the Beast as seen in Revelation 13:3. The outwardly-manifested form of global socialism will be initially seated in this Neo-Roman Empire, but a divided Germany remained an obstacle in the finalization of the healing of the last world empire.

The two horns of the United States and England have effectively and methodically followed the blueprint orchestrating the world into a New World Order. Little by little the construction of the global edifice arises. The plan of the Internationalists is to have their representative seated upon the throne of world government by the year 2000. All diligence is being applied to this end.

The False Prophet, with all the authority of the Beast uses three methods of power and control for bringing the world into this New world Order. The next section deals with each of these methods. They are the tools of the Agent of Antichrist, Architect of the New World Order.

Chapter Twenty Four

FIRE FROM HEAVEN

He performs great signs, so that he even makes fire come down out of heaven to the earth in the presence of men.

Revelation 13:13

Orville and Wilbur

When nine and twelve year old Orville and Wilbur went out to play, little did they realize that their playful discoveries would revolutionize the world and drastically alter the way men would think about time and space.

Orville and Wilbur Wright stumbled into the hidden mysteries of flight. Dreams that men had dreamed for thousands of years were realized by the initial discoveries of these two unusual boys. The hidden wisdom that God had reserved for birds' mastery of flight was now unfolding to the Wright brothers. The heavens, which belong to the birds, were now to be shared with man.

Many reasoned, if the heavens belong to the Lord, then man has no business in the sky or outer space. After all, if God had intended man to fly, He would have given him wings like a bird. If that line of reasoning was carried out, then, since man was not given wheels for legs, he shouldn't drive cars.

If man's incredible intelligence is taken away, how could it be said he is made in the image of God? The real issue, then, is not so much what is known about the principles of the universe, but, rather, what is done with what is learned. This is a matter of conscience.

The problem, of course, is that collectively man's record on his trek across the annals of history is very poor when it comes to the use of knowledge.

Although the world has technologically progressed, especially in the last 100 years, there has been an explosive increase in moral and environmental degeneracy. Has technology, then, created a better human race? The answer is No! Man is just more sophisticated in his route toward debasement, but this is not an indictment against technology. Man without an internal conscience adjustment will inevitably turn what is meant for good into evil. This is the peculiar nature of the human race.

The Knowledge of Flight

When the knowledge of flight arrived around the turn of the century, it was not considered by the masses to be of any great significance. People did not believe much would come of it. Yet, within a few short years flight began to play an extremely important role in the first World War. Man had invaded the realm of birds, and now new possibilities lay before him. He had risen above his terrestial environment and seated himself in the seat of God. Flight!

It had taken thousands of years to arrive, but the unconquerable had been conquered. What was next, the moon? People scoffed at this notion. Flimsy little airplanes (Jennies) that were made of balsa wood and cloth could hardly be taken seriously. But more and more was learned. Soon airplanes were able to cross the Atlantic Ocean. A voyage that took months by boat could now be made in a day, or little more. The world was made smaller by one man of courage and bravery.

The momentous trans-Atlantic flight by Charles Lindbergh immortalized flight and made it the most exciting scientific breakthrough of its day. Both Europe and America were startled by the significance of this marvelous and heroic deed. Lindbergh was swamped by crowds and parades as the world marveled at the magnitude of his accomplishment.

The skies today are traversed with ease, as powerful jets move millions around the earth yearly. Today, 60 years later, Lindbergh's flight seems so small, but it was his flight that made a quantum leap in men's minds about the possibilities of flight. One of those possibilities was the utilization of flight for war

Nation Will Rise Against Nation

The imposing of one nation's will over another took on new possibilities with this technology. The idea of a Global Empire came under consideration in the mind of Adolf Hitler. Soon airplanes were armed with bombs. The world was at war. The airplane that was once made of cloth and balsa was now made of light weight metals and able to lift huge cargoes of weapons.

London and Poland were bombed by Hitler's Luftwaffe in his Blitzkrieg warfare. In return Germany was bombed by an armada of B-17s. Cities were literally incinerated by fire storms. Tens of thousands of people died, not by the explosions of the bombs, but by the intense fire that sucked up all the breathable air.

America discovered how to make nuclear weapons. During the war in the Pacific with Japan, nuclear bombs were dropped on Hiroshima and Nagasaki. The intense fires from the blasts created temperatures as great as those of our sun. The cities were totally destroyed by fire. People were burned beyond recognition. Many of those who survived still carry the awful scars in their memories and on their bodies from *the fire that came down*.

Vietnam experienced the finest technological advancement in fire storms when massive air raids were called down on the country's villages and forests. Napalm bombs wiped out mile after mile and village after village.

More recently, in the middle east war with Iraq, a great object lesson was served. What great fear was instilled in the nations through the awesome air supremacy the Western nations and the coalition forces displayed. Who would dare go to war with the world's ultimate police force? What people, what nation, after seeing the utter havoc wreaked upon Iraq would dare make a militaristic move against the combined forces of the United Nations? Fire would come down. What fear!

But the ultimate has yet to come, in the seizures of the utmost high ground.

The Ultimate High Ground

While military strategists re-think the necessity of airplanes in the face of the tremendous success of guided missile technology in Desert Storm, others are revising their thinking concerning Star Wars, or the Strategic Defense Initiative.

The Star Wars technology, the brain child of the Reagan administration, is being pushed again due to the success of Iraq's SCUD missiles in the Gulf War. The absolute safest defense against missile weaponry is laser technology.

When President Bush made his State of the Union address in January of 1992, he made it very clear that although there would be massive military cuts in the budget due to the end of the Cold War, there would be a continued progress towards completion of the control of the skies in the Star Wars system of the Reagan years. Inevitably the system, when it is finished, will be turned over to the United Nations for complete policing of the world. So the latest and greatest fire from heaven will be the high tech of Star Wars.

He who controls that system will militarily control the world, for he will have the *finest* technological ability *to call fire down from heaven..*

> And he performs great signs, so that he even makes fire come down out of heaven to the earth in the presence of men.
>
> Revelation 13:13

Chapter Twenty Five

THE IMAGE OF THE BEAST

The Agent of Antichrist is, of course, the second Beast of Revelation, Chapter 13. Who he is has already been revealed. He is dubbed the Agent of Antichrist because he is the one who fashions out a kingdom for the Antichrist.

The kingdom of the Antichrist is a Global World Government called the Beast. It has already been shown in the last chapter what the ultimate police force is for this kingdom of Satan (fire from heaven), but to control the world there must also be a vast communication system and mind control network. Everyone must march to the same drum beat. There must be a universal focal point. There must also be a universal economic system as shall be pointed out in the next chapter.

What is about to be disclosed in this chapter is the second tool that the False Prophet is using to deceive the world into accepting a Global World Government.

And he deceives those who dwell on the earth because of the signs which it was given him to perform in the presence of the beast, telling those who dwell on the earth to make an image to the Beast who had the wound of the sword and has come to life. And there was given to him to give breath to the image of the Beast, that the image of the Beast might even speak and cause as many as do not worship the image of the Beast to be killed.

Revelation 13:14, 15

In Revelation 13:14 the Image of the Beast comes into the picture after the healing of a fatal wound to one of the heads of the Beast, as noted in several places in Revelation 13. Since the various heads (they are world empires) of John's first Beast (seven in number) have been explained as: Egypt, Assyria, Babylon, Persia, Greece, Rome and the British Empire, the revived head will be that which comes out of the seven.

And the beast which was and is not, is himself also an eighth, and is one of the seven, and he goes to destruction.

Revelation 17:11

The emergence of the European Common Market is clearly the revival of the slain seventh head, or the Internationalist controlled British Empire, only in an expanded capacity. The hidden power of the British Empire truly was global in scope, and it also incorporated a loosely controlled European continent that will become more tightly controlled in 1993.

The Common Market began to arise immediately after the sword of WWII ostensibly killed the British Empire. The emergence of the Common Market nations was the period that initiated the healing of the wound which was fully consummated with the Berlin wall coming down and the reunification of Germany. This was the purported healing of the seventh head that was slain by the great sword, and the manifestation of the eighth head of John's Beast.

The Image of the Beast, according to Scripture, will occur after the healing of the wound and the resurrection of the Beast's seventh head. It can be seen from Scripture that the image could have been present as early as 1945-46 with the termination of WWII

What is the Image?

The Greek word that is used to explain the second tool of the False Prophet is *eikon*. [1] It simply means an idol. In the ancient world an eikon was usually a figure that was hand-crafted out of wood or metal. Often it was made in the likeness of an animal or bird. The idol of Molock, for example, had the head of a bull and the hands of a man. Many times idols were replications of demonic powers, and people would actually bow down and worship them.

Even the ancient Jews fell into this problem and were chastised by God when Aaron made a golden calf that the people demanded so they could worship it. When Moses, who had gone to Mt. Sinai to receive the Ten Commandments had come back, he ran smack dab into this revelry and became intensely angry. God, working through Moses, smote the people with a curse and thousands died. They had already broken the first and second commandments.

You shall have no other gods before Me.

You shall not make for yourself an idol, or any likeness of what is in heaven above or on the earth beneath or in the water under the earth. You shall not worship them or serve them.

Exodus 20:3-5a

God spoke about idols or eikons in His Law to man. Perhaps man's lack of attention to this one principle has set him up for the greatest deception the world has ever known.

The global worship of the Antichrist is the False Prophet's objective. But what does the word worship mean? The word worship in biblical Greek is best understood by the picture of one kissing the hand of a king with one's knee bent in submission while the king is seated on his throne. This is an accurate picture of worship. It means submission, adoration, reverence or awe. [2]

In order to evoke this kind of worshipful response from the global masses, the Agent of Antichrist gives the eikon of the Beast life and the ability to speak. There are two words that explain the word life in the Greek language. One is the word *zoe* and the other is the word *pneuma*. The word zoe is the word from which zoology comes, and it means animate life. Zoe is life that only God the creator can give. The word that is given to explain the life that the Agent of Antichrist gives is the word pneuma. This word pertains to spirit life or spiritual life. Spiritual life is given, but not zoological life. [3]

It is clear that the idol that speaks, which has spiritual life, appears after the fatal head wound of the first beast has been healed, and that it is a tool in the hand of the False Prophet that he uses to enslave the whole world in a One World Global worship.

Clearly the last great global empire was the British Empire, and after WWII the eighth head, or the ten nation confederacy, began to arise.

For the emergence of the ten nation confederacy to occur, the False Prophet, or the Agent of Antichrist, had to be present. Scripture teaches he is contemporary with the first Beast and he is the one whose function it is to build the final form of the Antichrist's system. It is he who through his tools builds the final form of the Beast. Since he must be on the scene, his tools must also be present, because he uses the tools to build the New World Order.

What is the Image of the Beast, the second tool of the Agent of Antichrist?

TV - The Image of the Beast

Since World War II television has reshaped the American psyche. In all areas, entertainment, politics, marketing, education, and the presentation of news, TV is the pervasive conveyor of our presuppositional psychological grid. It has relocated and replaced the marketplace, the soap box, the pulpit, and the family. Telemarketing has become a respected and accepted form of shopping. Next will be telebanking. Whether we want to face it or not, the television has retooled not only American, but world thought, and has shrunk the world to a global commune.

With the single exception of the workplace, TV is the dominant force in American life. We are rapidly being assimilated by television into a global One-World Culture. Because of TV the world has invaded our homes so that a man's home is no longer his castle, his retreat from the world. It is our marketplace, our political forum, our playground, our school, our theatre, our recreation, and our link to an escape from reality. It is the vice which reflects and shapes our assumptions, and a means of assaulting those assumptions. It cuts through every socio-economic class, every geographic and cultural diversity. And it is the single binding thread of this country, the one experience that touches young and old, rich and poor, learned and illiterate. A country which was too big for homogeneity, filled by people from all over the globe without any set core of values, America never had a unifying bond. Now we do. Now it is possible to answer the question, What do Americans do? They watch TV.

And how much TV do they watch? The average American family watches the television set for an astounding six to seven hours per day. [4] That means the average child is spending more time watching television than he is going to school. In the 1980s there were over 150,000,000 TV sets that were turned on for an average of seven hours a day. By the early part of the next century it is possible, given the continued growth, that we will spend more hours watching TV than the hours given to sleeping.

We already know the average citizen spends one-fourth his waking hours in front of the television. [5] The only activity that takes more of our childrens' time is sleeping. There is no question that TV holds unparalleled power over America; more than schools, parents and churches.

George Gurban, Dean of the Annenberg School of Communication of the University of Pennsylvania, put it this way:

> In only two decades from 1946 to 1966 of massive existence, television had transformed the political life of the nation, had changed the daily habits of our people, had molded the style of the generation made overnight. TV had made global phenomena out of local happenings; redirected the flow of information and values from traditional channels to centralized networks reaching into every home. [6]

In other words, TV has profoundly affected what we call the process of socialization, which is the process by which members of one species interact.

By it's reach, TV is so pervasive that it can alter the American idiom overnight. Who can deny the socio-idiomatic phrase, "Where's the beef?" It swept the nation. TV has altered the eating and sleeping habits of most Americans. It has kept them up later at night, but has also kept them home. It has broken the traditional patterns of how children learn about the world. Television has altered the shape and speed of our knowledge of the world.

In the 1930s even as national radio grew, the mass circulation magazines were a centerpiece of American life for learning the news of the world, and for escaping from it. But by the time network TV was just twenty-five years old, the dominant weekly magazines, such as Life, Colliers, and Saturday Evening Post, had all died out. The most widely circulated magazine was TV Guide.

The sheer power and reach of this medium is one reason why we understand so little about it. Its swift conquest of America can be linked in large measure to the fact that TV as an instrument reflected one of the populace's most insistent desires, to be left alone. In 1946, there were 7,000 TV sets in America. In 1947 there were 178,000, with an estimated audience of one million. [7] In 1948, Milton Berle began his run on NBC, which helped explode production to 975,000 TV sets. One year later, 3,000,000 were made. By late 1949, TV drew 41% of the radio audience. This new medium, by accident more than design, was in the hands of relatively few people. And less and less by accident, these few people found themselves relatively free from effective control and accountability. This system had grown and taken shape in large measure because the invention had created new categories of reality. New sources of power that the government could not even contemplate until they were firmly in place. By mid-century, TV had conquered America. [8]

In one sense, we had expected it all along, in another sense, we never knew what hit us.

Chapter Twenty Six

TELEVISION - SNOW WHITE'S POISONED APPLE

J ust how close are we to the return of Christ? How can we see the times and know for sure when that event will take place? Jesus himself reminded us that we were to watch and pray. He warned that we were not to fall asleep with regard to the reality of His second coming. Sleep, of course, is characterized by simply being unconscious.

Today not only is the world unconscious of the impending return of Christ, but so is the church (Snow White). The world's unconsciousness is best explained by the Scripture where people are saying,

> Where is the promise of His coming? For ever since
> the fathers fell asleep, all continues just as it was from
> the beginning of creation.
>
> 2 Peter 3:4

The church, on the other hand, is like the famous story of Snow White. When she was offered the poisoned apple, and took a bite she fell into a deathlike sleep.

In our time it can be said we have no prophet to show us our signs. The enemy has laid siege to the temple. The poisoned apple God's people have bitten into is television. The poison, continues to spread a deadening sleep over the church.

The Common Plague of Smut

Since cable TV has stolen significant numbers of viewers through pornography, the major networks will further loosen their moral standards in the 1990s attempting to regain those who have strayed from their influence. A new wave of immorality will sweep the nation and the world. With the onslaught of pornography projected at the viewing public, we are indeed headed into perilous times.

The Serial Killing

In the final hours before the execution of Ted Bundy, the infamous serial murderer in January 1989, Bundy spoke of the influence of pornography in his life, and its subsequent effect on his behavior. He attributed his serial killing to the powerful influence of pornography on him. If his self analysis is true, then we can expect an enormous wave of violence upon women in the very near future.

What is Morality?

Morality is simply the standard that operates on the human conscience to monitor and control human behavior. God placed within the human conscience ten spiritual laws. These laws were clearly defined to the Jews when the prophet Moses received them from God on Mount Sinai 5,000 years ago. These ten spiritual laws were known to the Jews as the Ten Commandments.

These laws reflect God's divine nature. Since these laws were placed within man, in this sense, mankind is created in the image of God.

When man deviates from these laws, or transgresses them, he loses sight of the fact he was created in the image of God and becomes even less than the animals, not equal with them, for while they are amoral, man is immoral.

Since every man is a transgressor of what he knows intrinsically to be good, he is caught in a trap. His failure to keep what he knows in his conscience creates guilt. The conscience of man monitors good and evil both externally and internally. That is, it was designed by God to screen thoughts that enter our mind through environmental effects, and it also monitors our personal thoughts that arise within.

When the conscience is operating in a healthy capacity it will reject immoral thoughts that are in conflict with the laws of God written on the inner conscience. Thus morality functions in direct relationship with human conscience. The human conscience, then, to be perfectly clear, is like the door to a castle. Once it is broken down, the castle can be overcome. Pornography is an attack on the moral conscience.

Morality based on God-given law was inscribed on the human conscience and was verified to the Jews on stone tablets. These laws clearly expressed God's standard of righteousness and form the basis of human morality. In the Western world this concept is expressed as the Judeo-Christian ethic.

The human conscience stands to defend the inner person, or the subconscious from the attack on morality. As human beings grow they are either reinforced in their conscience, thus defending their inner person, or they are inundated and eroded by the opposite forces that mitigate against this principle.

Since the world defines the inner person as the subconscious mind, it is hard to make a point as to what the spiritual implications are in this matter. Most people, including Christians, accept the notion that whatever isn't conscious mind is subconscious mind. They accept the world's definition as true. The fact of the matter is, that what men call the subconscious mind is actually a man's spirit. The attack upon morality is an attack on the door to a man's spirit. If the door (conscience) is broken in, the man's inner temple (his spirit) is assailed, and, as in Ted Bundy's case, possessed.

Since we are spirit encased in flesh, the attack on our spirit is an attack on who we are. It is an assault on our personal identity. Ted Bundy is a classic example of the war that rages over a man's temple. Bundy became the antithesis of what God intended for him to be.

How the Tool Works

TV has been seized by forces that long ago began to, on a massive scale, break down the foundation of Western Civilization. The Judeo-Christian ethic must, in the eyes of the world planners, be overthrown in order to create a One-World Government. The stakes are high as more and more people bite into the forbidden fruit of TV's slide into smut.

To bring this into focus, it must be seen that if there is to be a final hour of organized lawlessness, it must begin with a total breakdown of God-defined morality so that men might be conformed to a global empire. Since the founding fathers of this great nation developed the Constitution based on a Judeo-Christian ethic, this country remains an obstacle in the plans for a new world order. If ever one wanted to make a case for a restraining force, America would be a good topic of conversation. Take America out of the world as a Christian nation and watch what happens. But this is exactly what TV is doing to this country. The Judeo-Christian morality is sinking fast. Destroying Christianity is exactly what the New World Order wants.

The New World Order Morality

This empire will not be based on laws of conscience placed there by God, but quite the contrary.

TV is quickly, within forty-five years, doing the job quite well. It is the major tool being used to reshape the world from the Judeo-Christian ethic into a new International standard that is not based on God's original intent for how man should judge thought or behavior. It could be said that the basic spirit of TV with fewer and fewer exceptions, is Antichrist.

Chapter Twenty Seven

THE LAW

When God gave the Jews the Law (Ten Commandments) through Moses, He was placing before them the mirror of their own conscience. Since God's laws are written within every man, the laws that were given to Moses were merely the reflection of a man's conscience. What was the purpose? The Law was given to bring clarification to a man's conscious mind. This explanation of God through law was both good and bad. It was good in that it declared He was selecting a people for Himself, and revealing to them His nature expressed in Law. It was bad, however, in that it laid out a standard for those chosen ones that was virtually impossible to live out.

The Law being perfect, because it was handed down by a perfect God, when imposed on people, was unlivable. The Law created a contrast between the perfect morality of a righteous

God and man, who no matter how hard he tried could never live this Law perfectly. Thus the Law expressing holy and righteous characteristics of God, became a curse. The Jews, who were called to live the Law, found themselves with the incredible dilemma of constantly having to deal with the notion of sin, or transgression of the Law.

How could these laws that rule the conscience, having been reinforced by the Ten Commandments on stone tablets, also show man to be a transgressor? Without a clear understanding of man's true predicament, every man would be schizophrenic because on the one hand the human conscience agrees with the Law given by Moses, but on the other hand, man cannot live by the Law. Man is both like God, in that his conscience shows the work of the Law, and like the Devil in that he tends to be against the very things he agrees are right and proper in his conscience.

Mental Disease

What does all this mean? The only explanation of this dialogue is to concede the fact that man's conscience isn't strong enough by itself to control a man's behavior. The paradox of conscience and a man's natural behavior that daily functions in contradiction to conscience, is the very source of most mental disease.

When God gave the Law (Ten Commandments) to the Jews He actually gave an unlivable standard. Wasn't that cruel? Why did He do that? He did that to clearly point out that man's nature had become estranged from God. God's ways are not nearly the ways of man. God's thoughts are much higher than man's thoughts.

God's purpose was not only to show the contrast between God and man, but the impossibility of any man attaining to the likeness of God by the sheer power of obedience to His Law. The Old Testament Law only made man more mindful of his moral inability. The Law as a covenant could never bring man into perfection. When we say a man is only human, we are saying he is not perfect. He's only human.

But how could God accomplish His plan to bring man to the point where he can perfectly obey and live the perfect Law?

The Atonement

When God gave the Law He knew man could not live up to its lofty standards. He gave the Law to make man mindful of his sortcomings, or sinfulness. However, along with the Law, God instituted the animal sacrificial system as the atonement principle to make amends for man's inability to live up to the standard of the Law. Although the animal sacrificial system was rudimentary in teaching man about justice, the sacrificial system was established to point to the fact that when a transgression of the Law occurred, either individually or corporately there had to be a penalty assessed to that particular transgression.

If a man committed murder, he was to die himself. If there was adultery, then a punishment for that sin was to be meted out. But to then approach God after a transgression, there also had to be the spilling of the blood of animals. The animal sacrifices required a priesthood to administrate the religious ordeal. The tribe of Levi was selected for this special responsibility. Does it sound like God is a blood thirsty God?

It is the holiness of God that requires the satisfaction for the transgression of the Law. The straying from the obedience to the Law was, and is, a depletion from the life of God. In order for man to be in right standing with God, once again there had to be the remitting of that sin. The expiation of that sin was achieved through blood. "For it is the blood by reason of the life that makes atonement" (Leviticus 17:11b).

The Law and animal sacrificial system were instituted only to instruct, and lead toward a better and more perfect contract with God. This is the New Covenant.

The New Covenant

The Law could not bring man's conscience into perfection, because the atonement for sin was a yearly ordeal, therefore he was constantly in remembrance of his transgressions. His conscience was continuously in discord with his behavior. Since man knows intrinsically the Law, his need is not legal knowledge, but rather power to enable him to live above the motions of disobedience within himself that operate against his conscience. Since the old Law needed the blood of animals yearly to bring about the remission of sin, God brought in His Son Jesus as a more perfect sacrifice, and through His blood man could finally have a once and for all atonement principle.

Through proper understanding and response to the New Covenant mankind can be free from mental disease, since mental disease is almost always the result of suppressed guilt. Guilt, of course, is the feeling upon the conscience that occurs when one violates the Law. If proper response to the atonement through Christ's blood is not invoked, then guilt is shoved down through the door of the conscience into the human spirit (subconscious). Mental disease is a legal problem with God that requires a payment against a violation of God's Law. The problem is complicated in that in God's court you are guilty when you violate the Law. But when an appeal is made to God on the grounds of the Blood of Jesus Christ (the New Covenant), quickly there is an immediate release from guilt.

Television and it's assault on the human conscience through the portrayal of immorality must be cautiously monitored. Our liberty in Christ must not be an occasion for license. We must carefully screen our T.V. viewing.

This particular section has dealt with TV, one of the three tools that the False Prophet is using to organize the world into the Global World Empire. Television is clearly an instrument in the hands of the Global Planners.

Chapter Twenty Eight

HERE IS WISDOM

A nd he provides that no one should be able to buy or to sell, except the one who has the mark, either the name of the beast or the number of his name.

Revelation 13:17

Jesus had much to say about money and riches. In fact, throughout the Scriptures many references speak of the power and transient nature of the riches of this world. Two examples are:

When you set your eyes on it, it is gone. For wealth certainly makes itself wings, like an eagle that flies toward the heavens.

Proverbs 23:5

> When you sit down to dine with a ruler, consider
> carefully what is before you; and put a knife to your
> throat, if you are a man of great appetite.
>
> Proverbs 23:1, 2

In other words, wealth can buy people. Money has the power to make men compromise their values.

The Antichrist Will Master Money

The coming world ruler, the Antichrist, will not only gain the mastery over mammon, he will be the consummate money manager when he ends up with all the gold, silver, costly stones, and treasures.

> But instead he will honor a god of fortresses, a god
> whom his fathers did not know; he will honor him
> with gold, silver, costly stones, and treasures.
>
> Daniel 11:38

> But he will gain control over the hidden treasures of
> gold and silver, and over all the precious things of
> Egypt.
>
> Daniel 11:43

When Jesus spoke on wealth he used the term mammon of unrighteousness. The word *mammon* in the ancient world meant riches, akin to a Hebrew word signifying to be firm, steadfast, hence, that which is trusted. [1]

> No one can serve two masters; for either he will hate
> the one and love the other, or he will hold to one and
> despise the other. You cannot serve God and mam-
> mon.
>
> Matthew 6:24

In other words, one is either serving God or money. He either puts his trust in one or the other.

During the temptations of Christ in the wilderness, Jesus was offered the kingdoms of the world and all their glory by the prince of this world, Satan. There was a catch in the offer. Jesus had to first bow down and worship him. Jesus passed on the deal, but someone will succumb, or already has, to that temptation, and take the Devil up on it.

When that time and day finally comes, the means for world control will come through the concentration and accumulation of wealth or mammon. The god of this world is mammon, and he who controls mammon will control the world.

Since 2 Thessalonians 2:1-12 teaches the coming of the day of the Lord will be preceded by the Antichrist, the forces pressing the world toward the New World Order will be noticed in the place where wealth is accumulating and concentrating. When the final and complete mastery of wealth is accomplished, Antichrist will soon appear, and the failure of mammon will follow.

Scripture instructs the faithful to:

> Make friends for yourselves by means of the mammon
> of unrighteousness; that when it fails, they may re-
> ceive you into the eternal dwellings.
> Luke 16:9

When mammon fails those who put their reliance in it will be enticed into *a new economic system*.

The New Global Economic System

The new system, as predicted in Revelation will no longer have any medium of exchange that man historically has been accustomed to using. What is coming is a total departure from anything man has ever known in the transacting of goods and services. There will be absolutely no exchange currencies such as dollars or coin or gold or silver. It is spoken of in the book of Revelation, as a system where only a mark is utilized.

> And he causes all, the small and the great, and the rich
> and the poor, and the free men and the slaves, to be
> given a mark on their right hand, or on their forehead,
> and he provides that no one should be able to buy or
> to sell, except the one who has the mark.
> Revelation 13:16, 17

Human nature is a strange thing. Usually people do not like to make changes in their lives unless there is a tragedy or a catastrophe of some sort. Since people naturally resist change, they will especially not favor changes in the way business is transacted today.

It is because of this human trait that the coming cashless economy is being foisted on the peoples of this country and the world gradually. It's coming is hardly being noticed. It is being phased in through the current electronic funds transfer and debit cards.

In order for its final form to be imposed, however, there will in all probability be a great depression or world banking collapse. As the United States debt continues to soar over four trillion dollars, and the federal budget deficit continues to climb, the reality of just how close we are to a collapse is not hard to see.

The most recent changes in East Europe signal drastic economic realities in the West. Now that the cold war has come to an end there is no longer the necessity for extensive military armaments. In the middle of the Gulf War the U.S. Department of Defense met with the U.S. Senate and discussed massive military cuts.

As the de-escalation in military spending began, the United States economy continued to sink into a recession. Thousands and thousands of jobs were lost as the country edged away from a war based economy.

When President Bush in his State of the Union address on January 28, 1992 announced further cuts in the military expenditures, it further exemplified the fact that this country is moving further away from a war based economy.

When They Say Peace, Peace

In order for there to be a replacement for the war-based economy, there will have to be a new economic base. The current reason (1992/93) for the loss of jobs in the United States is directly related to the scaling back of the war industries. The war based system is the pump that causes the rest of the economy to hum along. Now that there have been decisions to cut back the war industries, where will the new jobs come from? How will these war-based industries be replaced?

There are only two possibilities: Development and creation of jobs to offset the losses from the reduction of the war based economy must come either from an economic system based on outer space, or on environmentalism. Since the technological development of outer space industries is very expensive and highly technical, the answer for the new international economy will be, and now is, the emerging ecological environmentalism that is becoming so pervasive.

While the United States adjusts from its war based economy to the New World ecologically based economy, there will be tremendous economic wind shear. This is the price of peace.

As the unemployment rate increases, and massive loans are made to keep the economy going, great inflationary forces will be set off again. When business grinds to a halt due to hyperinflated and worthless dollars, people will gladly accept anything to get the show going again. They will accept a new world economic system that is cashless.

Justification for a Cashless System
The Great Works of Cainism

There are in the world today a great many distressing problems that a cashless system would seemingly correct and thus make such a system justifiable and reasonable:

1.   Without cash the International Drug Cartel could not operate and would fold overnight. A cashless society run by a mark on the hand or the forehead would almost totally eliminate this the world's greatest social problem. Without cash local and domestic growers would not be able to sell their goods.

2.   Since drug money cannot be taxed there is an economy functioning with huge fortunes accumulating within the drug cartels, and the money barons cannot regulate it.

3.   The people of the U.S. would do almost anything to stop the flow of drugs due to their destructive effect on the youth.

4.   The price tag to fight drugs through military expenditures would be cut to almost zero.

5.   As technology progresses, almost any novice today with the right equipment can counterfeit currency. During WWII millions and millions of bogus dollars were printed in Eastern

Europe and flooded into the market, causing great damage to our economic system. The destruction of a country's currency is a form of warfare. A mark that would eliminate cash would safeguard against the counterfeit currency problem, which will become worse with more sophisticated copying machines.

6.   Credit card fraud, which is now amounting to tens of billions each year, and the subsequent wrecking of people's credit through stolen cards would be totally eliminated.

7.   The uncontrolled influx of illegal immigration that destabilizes economic systems would almost totally stop. Remember, no one can buy or sell without a mark. And those coming into a country would be instantly tracked and found.

8.   In every nation there is an underground economy that goes untaxed. Hundreds of billions of dollars flows through the underground economic system in the U.S. alone. The underground economy in other nations is the dominant system in the economy. How does a nation pay its debts without taxation? And how can a government tax monies that cannot be tracked?

The following Associated Press release was published on October 8, 1989 in the San Diego Blade Tribune:

GOVERNMENTS ALARMED OVER GROWTH OF INFORMAL ECONOMIES
by Stan Lehman

SAO PAULO, BRAZIL (APS)

Underground economies typified by merchants selling goods on street corners are growing in South America, draining billions of dollars in taxes and other revenues from financially troubled governments.

But peddling goods, often smuggled, from fold-up tables on streets is the only way many South Americans can survive rising taxes, eroding wages and entrenched bureaucracies.

"The only way to earn enough to feed your family is to be self-employed and ignore the government, its red tape and its taxes," said Claudio Tavares on a busy street corner in downtown Sao Paulo, where he sells cheap disposable lighters and ball point pens, earning five times what he did as an office assistant.

Even self-employed professionals such as doctors, dentists, lawyers and psychologists are going underground. Not far from

Claudio Tavares' corner a dermatologist in an elegant private clinic tells a patient his bill will be 50 new cruzados (about $15) if the patient wants a receipt for tax records; without the receipt it's 37 new cruzados ($11).

The underground network provides millions of jobs, and extra income for the otherwise unemployed, but experts say the gross national product of many countries would grow 50% or more if underground economies were counted.

The informal economy "dodges direct taxation, but uses public schools and roads," the First National Bank of Boston said in a recent newsletter distributed in Brazil. "It avoids massive paperwork, government inspection, and the burden of dealing with 38 government entities to make simple business decisions." The bank estimated "an additional 30, 40, or even 50 percent of extra economic activities are out there bubbling away and contributing to a much more sizeable gross national product."

Economist Nelson Barrizelli of the University of Sao Paulo sees government as the reason for the growth of the informal economy. "The government, with its interventionist and highly centralized economic policies, is a virus that attacks the country's economic organism," he said in an interview. "The informal economy represents the antibodies society creates to protect itself from this virus." Barrizelli, who recently concluded a study on Brazil's underground economy, calculated it was about half the size of the country's official GNP, put at nearly $350 billion.

Some examples of this problem in the U.S. are:

Coin operated businesses such as laundromats can escape a great deal of taxation. How does a tax collector collect taxes on the cash that comes in on the untraceable number of times a washing machine or dryer is used during the course of a month?

A man in Oregon goes to a lumber mill and picks up the ends of some fir trees, chops them up, and sells them as firewood for $90 a cord. He takes the money, puts it in his pocket and goes his way. Since the transaction is totally in cash, there is no possible way the tax collector can get the tax from the $90.

A cash business avoids detection, and there are thousands of these types of businesses operating in an underground economy. A cashless economic system eliminates this secret flow of currency.

9.   A cashless system would eliminate a great deal of crime where the motive was cash. Think of it! All kinds of crime eliminated as money becomes virtually impossible to steal. There would no longer be bank robberies, skimmimg of funds, diverting of money. Sophisticated white collar crime would be no more. The economic system would be perfect. The justification for a cashless economy becomes very self evident when we look at the deteriorating conditions of society.

10.   The Federal Debt. If a man gets far over his head in debt, he has to declare bankruptcy. When this happens he has to start over again. After all, you can't get blood from a turnip. The same is true for a country.

The federal debt is so enormous that there is simply no way it can be paid back. Every year the compounding interest and continued borrowing to finance the annual budget deficit worsens the problem, which the new monetary system will eliminate. It will streamline the old nation states' system that simply doesn't work any longer.

The third world nations are already set for any kind of change that will bring them out of their hopelessness; especially nations like Brazil and Argentina that are buried under a mountain of debt they cannot meet the interest service on, let alone pay back. The U.S. is coming to that point as well.

11.   One of the greatest social and political problems of this decade is the issue of health care. Although the United States has the greatest health care system in the world, as of 1993, over 35 million people in the United States are without affordable health care protection. When the taxation problem is solved here and in other countries through the elimination of the underground economy, the amount of money to finance a universal health care program will immediately materialize. All it will take to have access to health care, here or anywhere else in the world, is to take the Mark, since it establishes you as a participant in the New World Order Economic Program.

Cainism Will Bring Global Peace

The most appealing aspect of the Mark will be a great reduction in the threat of war. Since many, if not most, wars come from the love of money, eliminate money and eliminate most wars and crimes. The people of the world will see this idea as the greatest boon to peace the world has ever known. The trade off, which is the total loss of privacy, they will reason, will be more than worth it. Anyone who doesn't go along with the idea will be viewed as unprogressive and a war monger, an enemy of the state. How could they not want peace? The pressure to conform to the new economic system will be enormous. It will be the peace movement that heralds the coming of this cashless society. Their cry will be peace and safety.

The people today who live in the great cities literally fear for their lives. The streets are unsafe. Muggings, rape, murder are the order of the day, and the night. Try wearing the colors of the local street gangs and see what happens. The people of the great cities are ripe for any reasonable answer. The people of earth are weary of conflict and poverty. All that is needed is a round of massive inflation and the new system will flow in on the cries of the people. The new world economic system will make the world safer.

Chapter Twenty Nine

LASER SCANNING SYSTEMS FOR SUPERMARKET AUTOMATION

Here is wisdom. Let him who has understanding calculate the number of the beast, for the number is that of a man; and his number is six hundred and sixty-six.

Revelation 13:18

When the universal product code was invented and introduced in 1973 by IBM (a Rockefeller owned corporation) there were five variations of the code, classed as A, B, C, D, and E. The A and E versions are most commonly used in grocery applications. Its primary purpose at the time was simply daily inventory control. This eliminated the need for large, or even small, grocery stores to go through the tedium of counting what was left on the shelves after each day's business. One could merely take stock by punching in the request to the computer, which calculated the day's business. [1]

Since that time, however, some innovative ideas for new uses of this invention have surfaced along with some very penetrating insights into just how the bar codes operate.

The Universal Product Code (UPC)

There are three major features of the UPC symbol:

1. The encodation uses varying width intervals of bars and spaces. This eliminates sensitivity to ink spread and allows the symbol to be read by scan lines not perpendicular to the bars. [2]

Fig. 1 UPC symbol showing width intervals for bar codes

2. The symbol can be read as two halves by the laser scanner beam and then combined in the computer system to yield the full 12 digit code.

Product   Manufacturerer
ID Number   ID Number

Fig 2 Two halves of UPC symbol

3. The size of the UPC symbol may be as large as 200% of the normal size, or as small as 80% of the normal.

0 16000 66210 4

Guard	Product	Center	Mfr ID	Guard
Bar	ID Number	Bar	Number	Bar

Fig. 3 UPC symbol enlarged to 200%

Figures 1, 2, and 3 illustrate a standard UPC symbol, which is the machine readable representation of the UPC code. A standard symbol consists of parallel light and dark bars of varying widths accompanied by numeric characters printed below each data character. The numeric characters are not readable to the computer, since it only reads the bar codes. The numeric characters are for human consumption, and represent the data which are encoded with the bars.

The left side of the symbol begins with a white margin and the guard bars (see Fig. 3) followed by the encoded number system character. This character is usually identified with a human readable character immediately outside the left margin. The system character is followed by five characters. These characters represent the number of each particular product. Then in the middle are the center bars, or the centerband, which are followed by five more characters representing the manufacturer number. The five data characters are followed by the guard bars and then the white margin. [3]

It is very critical to focus on the understanding that the computer does not know numbers as we know them. The computers, with incredible speed, calculate on the binary values of 1s and 0s.

The data bars of the UPC carry specific coded information on the product identification information, left side of UPC, and carry manufacturer identification information, right side of UPC.

The guard bars are, however, different in function than the data bars. The guard bars actually operate the computer. *They are computer programming characters.* They actually tell the computer when to start and stop picking up the data information. [4]

Of vital importance is the binary value of the guard bars. In Figure 4, on *the right side* of the UPC, the first data character next to the center bar is the data character with the equivalent numeric value of six. If you look at the design of that character it is exactly the same width as the guard bars. [5]

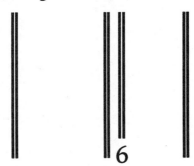

Fig. 4 UPC width design of guard bars

The light line then space and then another light line conforms exactly to the dimensions of the guard bars. Remember, the computer does not know numeric values, only binary values. So, when the electronic scanner goes over the marks on each package as you check out from the grocery store, it is only seeing 1s and 0s. This is also true of the guard bars. The computer is seeing the guard bars in the language of 1s and 0s. [6]

The Numeric Value of the UPC Guard Bars is 6-6-6

The most amazing thing is that although the guard bars encoded with 3 and 5 modules as 1-0-1 and 0-1-0-1-0 they operate on the same root as the data character 6 which is configured with

7 modules. The three bars within the UPC that operate the computer are all (in binary 1-0-1 and 0-1-0-1-0) or the eqivalent of the number of the data character six (See fig. 5).[7] Though the encodations are different the visable modules of 1-0-1 are the same.

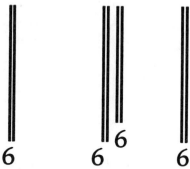

Fig. 5 Binary value of guard bars

The universal product code is a mark run by three sixes. It was designed as a boon to control and keep track of inventory for businesses. When the time is ripe, due to the many global problems, and the burgeoning world population, the mark will be applied to everyone for total world monetary control.

And he causes all, the small and the great, and the rich and the poor, and the free men and the slaves, to be given a mark on their right hand, or on their forehead, and he provides that no one should be able to buy or to sell, except the one who had the mark, either the name of the beast or the number of his name. Here is wisdom. Let him who has understanding calculate the number of the beast, for the number is that of a man; and his number is six hundred and sixty-six.

Revelation 13:16-18

The Application of 666

Here is a plausible scenario for how easily this technology can be adapted for a New World Order economic system. Everyone could be given the three programming characters (see Fig. 6)

These characters have been referred to as the guard bars and the center bar of the UPC. Each has a binary value of 1-0-1, which equates to the numeric value of 6. Ostensibly each person could be given the three computer programming characters 6-6-6.

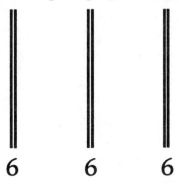

Fig. 6 The three UPC sixes

Each person could have three sixes which access the computer, and specific information concerning who they are and where they live (see Fig. 7). Then each could be given an electronic banking number.

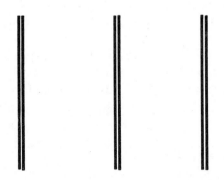

Fig. 7 Preliminary framework for personal ID number

As can be seen above, the three sixes could serve as the computer programming characters. Then in Fig. 8 the beginning bar codes of data are entered on the left side of the UPC. The data that have been added are 110 and 619.

The number 110 is the corporate ID number of the United States and 619 is the telephone area code of San Diego. Every nation has a corporate identification number. The corporate ID number indicates the national corporate computer system containing the individual's location, in this example, the United States. The 619 number answers to a local area computer. So we have 6-110-619-6. Plausibly 619 could reference a local computer.

Fig. 8 Data for personal residence

The right side of the UPC could have the PIN (Personal Identification Number). Since it is the law that every soul born in the United States must have at the time of birth a Social Security number, the PIN in all probability will be linked to the S.S. number. Since each area code computer system can contain up to nine hundred and ninety-nine thousand names, it can be seen that almost one billion names can be stored in the 110 (United States) corporate numbers system. We have added a six digit modified Social Security number that hypothetically could answer to the San Diego area computer district.

Fig. 9 Completed personal ID number

Once the mark is filled in, we have a completed PIN which allows the individual to do away with all earlier forms of identification. The sixes used to operate the computer by the laser scanner are the universal computer access number.

With this new system, an individual can travel the world no longer having the need to carry a passport, driver's license, credit card, or money. No money?

When a purchase is to be made, the laser scanner could simply scan the merchandise at, say, the supermarket. Then with a hand-held scanner, scan the customer's hand or forehead (the mark will be on the hand or the forehead) for the necessary personal information for an electronic funds transfer from that person's electronic banking account. The electronic banking account will be linked directly to the individual's personal information on the right side of the UPC. With incredible speed the EFT (Electronic Funds Transfer) will deduct from the individual's electronic account and transfer the funds into the account of the store where the purchase has been made.

EFT technology is now being installed in gasoline stations, restaurants, super markets, and every kind of retail agency. In Southern California a prominent fast foods chain is using a company called Interlink. The system links certain local banks together in a banking network. The system will allow a bank card purchase for food in that restaurant. The system automatically deducts the purchase price of the food from the individual's bank account and transfers the funds to the restaurant's bank account. This system has been in place for many years as a forerunner of the coming 666 world-wide cashless system.

A cashless society is being phased in right before our eyes. With the use of a mark instead of a card, the system of EFT will become even more streamlined. When a mark is invisibly laser tattooed on the hand or the forehead, there is no fear of misplacement or theft of credit or debit cards. The mark's PIN number can never be forgotten since it is permanently on the flesh. When all the technology is in place and all the computers are linked, the mark will be usable world-wide.

Many will invariably ask the tempting question, "When will this all happen? How long?" All it will take to bring about this new economic system is a banking failure. With the savings and loan debacle we are well on our way.

The Red Sea of Worldwide Debt

It is hard to understand the financial predicament of the United States. When the national debt is over four trillion, and the yearly deficit seems to be running in excess of 250 billion, the interest and the debt continue to accumulate at frightening speed. What this means is that either we will have tax increases or inflation.

There is no other solution to this ever present crisis. Since both inflation and tax increases represent a greater burden on the people, the system will eventually fall by its own weight of debt. All the world follows the U.S.A., so what is true for America is true for the rest of the world. When the U.S. went into a depression in 1929, the whole world went into the depression with us.

The global drug problem, coupled with terrific domestic and third world debt, and now the environmental problems that are being highly propagandized, are creating the climate for a new global world economic system.

The idea of a debit system as opposed to a credit system has already been with us in the west for many years. The American people have been blindly accepting the phase-in without a whimper. As the system is foisted upon America, some people are reluctant to pay their bills with electronic funds transfer, but they are powerless to fight the trend and the momentum of the direction the banking system is taking.

The Last Fulfillment

The coming world economic system will be just as the Bible predicted two thousand years ago. It will be a cashless system run by a mark that will be placed on the hand or the forehead.

The mark will be mysteriously run by three sixes and no one will be able to buy or sell except the one who has taken the mark. Certain destruction will come upon all those who take the mark for this is the ultimate economic system of the Antichrist and the Beast. Those who resist the mark are the ones that will have to live like vagabonds on the earth. These people will be made up of Christians, the chosen of God, who refuse Satan's government, and criminals that refuse to be involved in the system.

These insights should make it clear that we are in the time of the end, and that the Antichrist is nearer than ever. This tool of the False Prophet is the final economic system that is now being phased in and to be put in place, bringing about world economic control of all the people. A New World Order demands a New World Economic System.

Chapter Thirty

THE KING OF THE WORLD

The final chapter in this conspiracy against Jehovah and man will be the attempt of the coming Antichrist to set up the ancient throne of King David in Jerusalem, and establish himself as the King or the President of the World.

Why the Throne of David?

The throne of King David has great eternal significance and any Bible student knows that the throne of David is the sole possession of the Lord Jesus Christ. Jerusalem is to be the location of the seat of the throne of God on earth during His Millennial reign. The forces of evil will attempt to circumvent God's plan by establishing the *man of lawlessness* in place of the rightful heir.

The coming return of the Lord Jesus Christ has been waited for and prayed over by the saints of God for almost two thousand years. Since the time that Jesus ascended from the Mount of Olives, the people of God have been awaiting the day when He would return and set up His earthly kingdom. It is odd indeed that millions of His people today do not realize that when Christ returns He will do away with the kingdoms of this world and set up His own kingdom, which will last for one thousand years, and He will rule it with a rod of iron (Revelation 2:27).

Before Christ returns, Satan, through the incredible strategy of the New World Order he has been busily shaping for centuries, will seek *once again* to seat himself in the place of the Most High. Isaiah reveals the first attempt to usurp God's throne in heaven, and now Satan will try for God's throne on earth. The throne of God on the earth is the throne of King David, (Isaiah 14:13).

When Christ walked on the earth, the original disciples expected an immediate restoration of the Kingdom of David, which they believed Jesus would then establish and rule (see Acts chapter 1). The disciples knew Him to be the Son of David, (Matthew 9:27). The true fact of the matter was that Jesus was not only prophesied in the Old Testament as the coming Son of David, but when He arrived on the scene some two thousand years ago, He clearly responded to that title.

Now as we approach the two thousandth year of New Testament times, the world is rapidly moving towards a Global World Political and Economic System, and yet there is no apparent king to run the show.

This coming Global system is a counterfeit millennial kingdom that Christ will destroy because it is in total contradiction to His prophesied Millennial kingdom. Prior to His return, however, there will come the great imposter, or the Antichrist, attempting to usurp Christ's position as heir apparent to King David. This entire system as we watch Europe rapidly come together, Eastern Europe moving toward Democratic forms of Government, and joining the Western world's economic system, should excite the hearts of every Christian, because these things must take place before Christ returns (2 Thessalonians 2:1-12).

To sum up: Jesus is the Son of David who will come to rule the world, and He will destroy this global world system that will have its initial locus in Western Europe, but will eventually remove to Jerusalem. It will be ruled for a short time by the usurper, Antichrist, who will attempt to lay claim to the ancient throne of David.

Who is the Antichrist?

In the Old Testament God used types as examples to foreshadow events that would occur in the latter years. In the case of the usurper who will come with the Global World Government, claiming himself to be God, there is an interesting Old Testament type. A careful study should be made so light may be shed on detecting the advances of the Antichrist.

Old Testament Parallel

The story centered around King David during the time when his kingdom was firmly in hand. It was the time when Israel was a unified nation, and not divided between north and south, but was actually in the height of its glory. But even though David's kingdom was seemingly under control, his immediate family was having some terrific problems.

The fundamental reason for the internal discord was due to the problems that arose out of David's concept of marriage. King David was a polygamist. Polygamy is the word used to explain the idea of a man having many wives. Though David was a man who loved God, and was a man who sought after the Lord more than any other, his desire for many women led to a tremendous problem within his own household. It seems strange that God never spoke to him on this matter, but allowed him to continue on in this grave mistake.

There came a time when a serious conflict arose amongst the children of his family. David had many sons and daughters from different wives. The problem arose out of the incestuous lust of David's son Amnon for David's daughter Tamar. Amnon was so strongly aroused for his half sister that he sought council from David's nephew Jonadab, a very shrewd man, and a friend of Amnon. Jonadab counseled Amnon on manipulating Tamar into a compromising position, and then taking her sexually by force (2 Samuel 13:1-14).

When the event came to pass, and Tamar was shamed, news of the rape came to Tamar's full-blooded brother, Absolom. As a result Absolom deeply hated Amnon. Absolom waited for his father, the king, to deal with the tragedy, yet David failed to act in any disciplinary way towards Amnon. Absolom continued to hold onto his hatred for Amnon, and reasoned that if his father would do nothing, then he would act (2 Samuel 13:24-39). After all, the Law of the Jews declared that:

> If there is a man who takes his sister, his father's daughter or his mother's daughter...it is a disgrace; and they shall be cut off in the sight of the sons of their people. He has uncovered his sister's nakedness; he bears his guilt.
>
> Leviticus 20:17

When the king delayed disciplining his son Amnon, Absolom made arrangements to kill his brother, taking the law into his own hands, he killed the one who defiled his sister.

Absolom fled Jerusalem and his father. He lived in obscurity for several years, but eventually returned to Jerusalem to seek the favor of his father. David, however, shunned his son. Then Absolom, feeling justified and self-righteous about taking Amnon's life, sought to usurp the throne of his father, David (2 Samuel 15:1-12).

It is an interesting exercise to speculate on the machinations of Absolom's inner reasoning. Perhaps he felt that his father was too old and couldn't execute sound judgement any longer. After all, didn't the law require action against Amnon? Or maybe he felt that underneath it all his father was really a weak man and couldn't act against his own family with the kind of ultimate punishment that the law required for a rape.

Whatever the reasoning and motivations, Absolom sought, through a conspiracy, to usurp the throne of David. Absolom the murderer now becomes Absolom the thief and usurper. Satan himself is characterized in the New Testament as a liar, a thief and a murderer. We see in Absolom now the characteristics of Satan the enemy of God and man, but displayed in a man. The Antichrist that is to come will have these same attributes.

Lucifer's Character

Satan, as he is revealed in the Bible, was once an archangel. Lucifer's character has not changed. His modus operandi in his hatred toward God is still the same. He formerly desired to usurp God's throne, and now his character and behavior is reenacted using Absolom as his pawn. Any willing human agent will do for the purposes of the "prince of the power of the air", as he is also called (Ephesians 2:2). In the time of King David, Absolom, his own son, was a prototype of the coming Antichrist.

Implications of the Assault

When the Lord Jesus came to the earth initially, He had to fulfill every prophecy spoken of Him. Most specifically, however, He had to be a descendant of the royal line of succession of the Kings of Israel. At the same time, He had to be born through immaculate conception by the Holy Spirit of the human race.

In other words, He had to be born of the seed of man and the seed of God at the same time. Hence, He would refer to Himself as the Son of Man and also the Son of God. Christ, however, could not have an earthly father, because the blood of the human race was tainted with a curse. Life is transmitted by the blood and the sin nature is passed on to each successive generation by the male side of the human race.

Christ, the incarnation of the living God, being the fullness of the Godhead bodily, could not have the sin nature of the human race and still be God (Colossians 2:9). By being of the seed of the woman, through Mary, and yet being immaculately conceived by the power of the Holy Spirit, God accomplished the task of not only fulfilling prophecy, but setting up the necessary ingredients for the rescue mission of the human race.

Mary was a descendent of King David through Nathan, David's son through Bathsheba, David's wife, and therefore in the lineage of the royal King David. Through Mary's ancestry Jesus obtained the title of Son of Man, and also Son of David.

Christ's Legal Inheritance

Jesus, however, would have had no legal claim to the earthly throne had it not been for Joseph. Joseph, His step-father, was the key to the legal claim of Christ to the throne of King David. Joseph was a descendant of David, too, only Joseph's line of ancestry proceeded from Solomon, from whom came the royal line of the kings. Therefore Christ's legal claim to the throne of David came as a result of the marriage of Joseph to Mary before Jesus was born. This marriage was necessary to enable Christ Jesus to be the legal heir to the throne of David even though Joseph was not the natural father of Jesus.

Furthermore, through Joseph *only* could the Lord Jesus become the legal heir to the throne (I Kings 9:5, 6). He could not be connected to the succession of the actual kings. In His humanity this had to come from Mary. This was due to another taint that was placed upon the kings at the time of King Jeconiah. This particular king was so evil that God had to literally take back a provision He had made because Jeconiah had transgressed to the degree that God could no longer keep his promise the original way He intended it. The legal rights could be conferred, but the literal seed would not descend. Of Jeconiah God says:

> Write this man down childless, a man who will not prosper in his days; for no man of his descendants will prosper sitting on the throne of David or ruling again in Judah.
>
> Jeremiah 22:30

Joseph had to have a connection to the royal lineage of Solomon to whom God had made a promise that an heir would be forever seated on his throne. Joseph's genealogy, as it is traced in the book of Matthew, ends with his connection to the royal lineage of King David through Solomon.

One last important thing; Joseph had to be wed to Mary prior to the birth of Jesus to confer this legal right of succession. Had Joseph delayed becoming Mary's husband until after Jesus was born, Jesus would have been illegitimate. By wedding Mary before the birth, Joseph became the legal father of Jesus, imparting to Jesus the legal right to the throne of David (Matthew 1:24).

Had Absolom succeeded, had the conspiracy supplanted King David, it would have prevented Jesus from coming to the earth. It is conceivable that God could have worked out another virgin birth through some other party. However, that would have made Jesus Christ the Savior and not the coming King.

We see here the operation of the foreknowledge of God and the absolute literal fulfillment of prophecy. God in His infinite knowledge and wisdom worked out through time that His Son be not only Savior of the world, but also the heir to the throne of King David.

It must be remembered that Satan's murder of Christ at the hands of the Romans and the Jews was because Christ claimed to be King. Satan seeks a throne and a kingdom, as we have seen. When the throne of David was assailed during David's lifetime by the adversary through human agency, and then again during Christ's lifetime, it becomes clear that this is Satan's purpose on the earth. He will try again, but this time by seating himself on the throne of A One-World Government.

Lucifer's Clear Pattern

Lucifer at one time was very close to God. He was the anointed cherub. It was through an insurrection that the attempt on God's throne came. It was through an agent whom God trusted, and who was given hallowed secrets of the Government of God (Isaiah 14:12-14). On earth in the person of Absolom, the same pattern occurred. A son whom his father trusted and deeply loved turned and sought through satanic inspiration the usurpation of the throne.

During the time Jesus walked the earth the pattern emerged again. This time the traitor was Judas, one of the original disciples (John 13:2, 3). The repetition of Satan's behavior makes the pattern clear. The Antichrist will arise from one who has been given great trust and power. It may come from one who is even now considered a Christian, or perhaps one from Jewish descent. "But instead he will honor a god of fortresses, a god whom his fathers did not know..." (Daniel 11:38). Certainly this Scripture indicates he will come from either of those two camps.

But just as God had Lucifer outflanked before, He still has all things under control. All these events are taking place in order to prove and test the people the Lord God has called unto Himself.

Chapter Thirty One

HOW THEN SHALL WE LIVE

Now that you have heard all of these things, what should be your response? How should I live out my life? What is my responsibility as a believer, as a disciple, as a citizen of America? What good is all this knowledge? What is God's intent with disclosing all these things to me?" These questions typically flood the mind of the hearer.

The Lord Himself spoke in these apocalyptic terms, but always pointing towards a positive anticipated end for the believing; the negative signs always pre-dating His return. Are these signs really negative?

It is the natural man that finds this information fantastic, fatalistic, and unbelievable. "It's so negative. Where is the peace and the hope?" one might ask. The spiritual man knows that no matter what happens, the Lord is his confidence. His trust is in the Lord Jesus Christ. It is the natural man that looks for ease and comfort. He has no place for the consideration of a world that offers no promise for a peace or hope that meets the expectation of his goals. The peace that the natural man seeks is that which the world gives. The spiritual man seeks the peace from God.

> Peace I leave with you; My peace I give to you; not as the world gives, do I give to you.
>
> John 14:27

In the face of all the external confusion and chaos, God's Spirit steadies our inner man with these promises. "I will never desert you, nor will I ever forsake you," (Hebrews 13:5). "The Lord is my rock," (Psalms 18:2).

> For momentary, light affliction is producing for us an eternal weight of glory far beyond all comparison, while we look not at the things which are seen, but at the things which are not seen; for the things which are seen are temporal, but the things which are not seen are eternal.
>
> 2 Corinthians 4:17, 18

"But when these things begin to take place, straighten up and lift up your heads, because your redemption is drawing near," (Luke 21:28).

These signs have been given by God so that through His perspective we would be enabled to discern the nearness of the coming of the Lord. What can be more encouraging for those who love His appearing than to see the fulfillment of biblical prophecy coming to pass right before their eyes? Praise God, the Kingdom is coming! We should be genuinely excited because the *Day of the Lord* is near.

It is only our flesh that gets in the way and fears the uncertainty of the world and the cataclysmic changes. If our hope and peace rests in the stability that the world has to offer we will suffer great loss and have great fear. The word of God teaches the disciples to grip the world loosely, not to tighten our hold on that which is failing for it will fail. If ever there were a time when people should be taking to heart the admonition to *love not the world* it is in this day, especially after hearing this revelation.

We are on the brink of what Scripture calls, perilous times. The One World Banking System is so close that even the most casual look at what is going on bears witness to this fact. All the saints should seriously reevaluate their relationship with the Lord and get their spiritual house in order. The King is coming!

We must leave dead churches and find churches where the Lord is truly visiting His people by the authentic presence of the Holy Spirit. We must not settle for mere lip service to the Holy Spirit, but where He is there is a genuine presence of God so that we know that we have touched the Living Hope. If we fail to contact God, or rather He to contact us, then we will look to the world for security and it's false peace and hope. The world's answer to man's essential needs is indeed empty. There is no hope in the world. There is only hope in Jesus Christ.

The Outward Response

What about our culture? Should we just give it up and let the current trends take their course? The message given in this book gives new insights into the world in which you live, a world in which there is not only God's church being prepared, but also where millions of people walk in great darkness.

Go open their eyes so that they might see clearly their need for a savior. Share with them where it is all going, and pray with them to accept the Lord. You have been given fresh insights into the Word. These insights are weapons for the tearing down of incredible strongholds; strongholds which exist in peoples' minds. Bring this Word to bear on people's minds by speaking it to them. Use your new weapons and fight against the bulwarks of the enemy. Do it now! The time is very short.

We must remember that "God so loved the world that He gave His only begotten son," (John 3:16). Christ wants us to fight a good fight. He wants us in the battle. We must also see that the people being used by the Devil to bring about a One World Government are loved by the Lord. We must raise the standard of Christ in every quarter.

In the secular schools we must stand against the false morality of the world. On the job we must tell the story to the unregenerate of why their taxes are so high, who is behind it all, and how they can become part of the solution. In government we must overturn immoral and ungodly laws that break down the structure of the nuclear family and tear at the core of society.

We must battle the gay and lesbian rights movements along with euthanasia and the women's movement, which are proponents of godlessness. We must get involved in putting an end to the drug problem. Where is the church? We need new troops. We must become more involved in the abortion issue, as many already have. We must be involved in every dimension of civic life. Where are the men to coach Little Leagues and basketball? Where are the mothers for Girl Scouts? We must get involved so that we can become all things to all men that we might win some.

The people of the world are looking for leadership in every area. We, God's people, must take the responsibility and aspire to fill the positions. After all, who is more qualified? We have the mind of Christ. What are we waiting for? Move ahead and be the answer! Leadership positions will place us in the arena so that we can tell the story of our Leader. There is no hope from the world. There is no lasting peace from the world. The answer is not there.

The Most Critical Factors

The information in this book should make you less inclined to be of this world, but retreating from it is absolutely not God's answer, nor His will. To be in, but not of it, does not mean to abandon it and run for the hills. The knowledge that the world is passing away should cause us to act as a preservative until Christ takes us out. Don't take yourself out before the Lord does.

The friction that comes from engaging the enemy in this final round of battle is God's plan for the restoration of our souls. We must learn that as we stand for the Lord, and model Christ in the face of Satan, we gain the Lord's character and nature. The battle enables us to become more like our King. We are perfected by faith in Christ. It is in the heat of battle that we must learn to trust in the Lord. This is His end time plan for the perfecting of the saints. Let us run to the battle line and engage the enemy.

Engaging the Enemy

It is not enough to fill all the positions of leadership where the lost can be won. Certainly the evangelization must go on until the Lord returns, and God's only hope for the lost is the out-stretched arm of the church. But we must remember that we are fighting a spiritual war. We must use spiritual weapons for that war. They are essential for our fight. It is at the point of spiritual warfare where there rests a delicate balance. The balance rests on prayer and external effort.

We simply must pray with all prayer. We must first engage the enemy in the spiritual realm. We engage the enemy and bind him with the use of the keys to the kingdom. Then, throughout the whole of the Bible, and specifically in the book of Ephesians we are instructed to put on the whole armor of God.

> Put on the full armor of God, that you may be able to stand firm against the schemes of the devil. For our struggle is not against flesh and blood, but against the rulers, against the powers, against the world forces of this darkness, against the spiritual forces of wicked-ness in the heavenly places. Stand firm therefore, HAVING GIRDED YOUR LOINS WITH TRUTH, and HAVING PUT ON THE BREASTPLATE OF RIGH-TEOUSNESS, and having shod YOUR FEET WITH THE PREPARATION OF THE GOSPEL OF PEACE; in addition to all, taking up the shield of faith with which you will be able to extinguish all the flaming missiles of the evil one. And take the helmet of salvation, and the sword of the Spirit, which is the word of God. With all prayer and petition pray at all times in the Spirit, and with this in view, be on the alert with all persever-ance and petition for all the saints.
>
> Ephesians 6:11, 12; 14-18

We must diligently use our authority as sons of God to war against Satan by binding him in the Name of Jesus. We must pray to God in Christ, model the person of Jesus, and speak the Word.

The plan is this. We must reach up continually to our Father in all matters, and trust in Him. We must know that the battle is essential so that Christ be fully formed within us. We are called to win the lost. Each aspect of God's plan must be in balance. Nothing works unless all aspects of the plan are being lived out together.

We should not fear this hour in which we live. This is the greatest time to be alive in all the history of the world. Jesus is coming again. The difficulty of these times serves to make us more like Him. Though we lose the world, we gain the Lord. To live in this era of human history there is great reward.

His Reward Is With Him to Give to Every Man

Millions of people depend on you to take your place, and to be ready to give an answer to anyone that asks you the reason of the hope that is in you. Go be fruitful! "In the world you have tribulation," Jesus said, "but take courage; I have overcome the world," (John 16:33).

The following statement by the prophet Habakkuk sets this whole work into proper perspective. Habakkuk was told by God of the coming day when the Babylonians would be raised up to overwhelm the world and displace Israel. God told him to write the vision down so that it would be very plain to anyone who would read it.

The knowledge of the coming judgement was unbearable to him, but this is what he wrote. This day is no different than that time and so these words apply.

I heard and my inward parts trembled; at the sound my lips quivered. Decay enters my bones, and in my place I tremble. Because I must wait quietly for the day of distress, for the people to arise who will invade us. Though the fig tree should not blossom, and there be no fruit on the vines, though the yield of the olive should fail, and the fields produce no food, though the flock should be cut off from the fold, and there be no cattle in the stalls, yet I will exult in the Lord, I will rejoice in the God of my salvation. The Lord God is my strength, and He has made my feet like hinds' feet, and makes me walk on my high places.

Habakkuk 3:16-19

Chapter Thirty Two

SUMMARY

This book has shed new light on an old topic. It has laid out the panorama of human history so that the reader can gain greater objectivity with a fresh Christian world view. It has been shown that throughout time the human race has been moving toward a One World Government, eventually to be ruled by a man who would claim to be the master of the human race: the Antichrist.

Step by step light has been shed on the world empires and powerful people that have arisen throughout time nudging the master plan along. With the death blow to the British Empire from the great world wars of the 20th century, the focus of this exposition shifted the spotlight onto the infamous False Prophet.

Since most theologians have been blinded by an incomplete understanding of the False Prophet the central thesis of this book has been to identify the False Prophet and his two horns as the

United States and Great Britain. Also, it was made clear that the False Prophet has immense power which he uses to set up the final system of the Antichrist called the Beast. The ten kings of the Beast system shall have world-wide impact, and be ruled by the Antichrist.

The spiritual purpose underlying this book is to retrieve and reactivate many believers who have succumbed to the temptations of the world and have lost their zeal for the Lord. The high ground of a Christian world view gives God's perspective on human history, and has the impact that disengages the love of the world, and prepares the heart for the King of Kings to rule and reign.

To God Be the Glory!

CHAPTER NOTES

Chapter 1:   The Last Stroke

1. Eustace Mullins, The Secrets ofthe Federal Reserve (Stauton, VA: Bankers Research Institute, 1985), 3.
2. Ibid.
3. Hal Lindsey, Late Great Planet Earth (Grand Rapids: Zondervan, 1970), 105.

Chapter 7:   The Mother of All Harlots

1. The Jewish Encyclopedia, 9:309.
2. Alexander Hislop, The Two Babylons (Neptune, N.J.: Loizeaux Brothers, 1916), 40-42.
3. Ibid, 75.
4. Ibid.
5. Ibid.
6. Woodrow, R., Babylon Mystery Religion, 153.

Chapter 8:   Tracking The Beast

1. PhilipMyers, Ancient History, Table of contents. Myers' book is a good exmple of many historical books that explain the evolution of the great empires.

Chapter 9:   Mystery Babylon

1. Hislop, The two Babylons, 41-45.
2. Ibid.
3. Ibid.
4. Ibid, 18-19.
5. Ibid, 12-19.
6. Ibid.
7. Ibid, 20-21.
8. Ibid.
9. Ibid.
10. Ibid, 41-45
11. Ibid, 30-32.

12. Ibid.
13. Ibid.

Chapter 10:   The Five Fallen Kings

1. World Book Encyclopedia (World Book Inc.: 1988), Egypt, 6:133-144.
2. Ibid.
3. Ibid.
4. Ibid.
5. Ibid.
6. Hislop, Two Babylons, 22.
7. Ibid, 38
8. Myers, Ancient History, 62-69.
9. Ibid.
10. Ibid, 38.
11. New Bible Dictionary (Grand Rapids: Eerdmans, 1967), 119.
12. Myers, Ancient History, 88.
13. Ibid, 93-94.
14. Ibid, 89.
15. John Walvord, Daniel-The Key to Prophetic Revelation (Chicago: Moody Press, 1971), 129-131.
16. Myers, Ancient History, 90-91.
17. Ibid, 95-97
18. Star, History of the Ancient World, 378-385.
19. Hislop, Two Babylons, 49-50.
20. Ibid.
21. Ibid, 48.

Chapter 11:   Rome

1. Harper's Dictionary of Classical Literature, 1387.
2. Star, Ancient World, 575.
3. Ibid, 576.
4. Ibid, 576-600.

Chapter 12:   The Seventh Head

1. World Book, V.2, the entire section on England.

2. John Reeves, The Rothschilds, Financial Rulers of the Nations, 167.
3. World Book, England
4. Ibid.
5. Des Griffin, Descent Into Slavery (Clackamas, OR: Emissary Publications, 1978), 26-27.
6. Des Griffin, Fourth Reich of the Rich (Clackamas, OR: Emmissary Publications, 1976), 41-45.
7. Ibid.
8. Anton Chaitkin, Treason in America (New York: New Benjamin Franklin House, 1985), 265-304.
9. Ibid.
10. Ibid.
11. Ibid.
12. Ibid.
13. Ibid.
14. Ibid.
15. Ibid.
16. Ibid.
17. Ibid.
18. Ibid.
19. Ibid.
20. Ibid.
21. Ibid.
22. Ibid.
23. Griffin, Descent, 26.
24. Nesta Webster, The French Revolution (Nesta Webster, 1919), 2-36.
25. Ibid.
26. Ibid.
27. Griffin, Descent, 26.
28. Ralph Epperson, The Unseen Hand (Tucson: Publius Press, 1985), 140.
29. Ibid.
30. Ibid.
31. Ibid.
32. Griffin, Fourth Reich, 88.
33. Epperson, Unseen Hand, 166 & 168.

Chapter 14:   World War I & II

1. John Robinson, Proofs of Conspiracy (Boston: Western Islands, originally published in 1798), 57-156.
2. Challenging Years, 189-197.
3. Griffin, Descent, 95-98.
4, Griffin, Fourth Reich, 124.
5. Griffin, Descent, 26-40.
6. Ibid.
7. Ibid.
8. Konrad Heiden, Der Fuehrer (Boston: Houghton Mifflin, 1944), 64-65.
9. Ibid, 5.
10. A. S. Sutton, Wall Street and the Rise of Hitler (Seal Beach, CA: 76 Press, 1976). The entire book is a record of the banking powers' arming of Hitler.

Chapter 15:   The Great Sword

1. Sutton, Wall Street, 67-76.
2. Joseph Carr, The Twisted Cross (Shreveport, LA: Huntington House, 1985), 36.
3. Heiden, Der Fuehrer, 1-18.
4. Cleon Skousen, The Naked Capitalist (Salt Lake City: 1970), 30. Lord Balfour worked within the Round Table's elite, including both Rhodes and Rothschild.
5. Heiden, Der Fuehrer, 65.
6. Ibid, 64.
7. Ibid, 528.
8. Ibid, 586-87.

Chapter 16:   The Satanic Resurrection

1. Griffin, Descent, 34-46.
2. Mullins, Secrets of the Federal Reserve, 1-2.

Chapter 18:   The False Prophet

1. W.E. Vines, Expository Dictionary of New Testament Words (London: Oliphant, 1940, Distributed by Revel), 1:222.

2.   W.E. Vines, Expository Dictionary of New Testament
Words, 1:89.

Chapter 19: History of the False Prophet
New Zion

1. Peter Marshall, The Light and the Glory (Old Tappan, NJ:
Revell, 1977), 106.
2. Ibid.
3. Ibid, 110-11.
4. Ibid.
5. Ibid.
6. Ibid.
7. Ibid.
8. Ibid.
9. Ibid, 270-309.
10. Charles Nroburn, Honest Money (Ashville, N.C.: New
Puritan Library, 1983), 8-9.
11. Ibid, 9-11.
12. Ibid.
13. Charles Norburn, Honest Government (Ashville, N.C.:
New Puritan Library, 1984), 10-11.
14. Norburn, Honest Money, 10-11.
15. Ibid.
16. Ibid.
17. Skousen, Naked Capitalist, 8-11.
18. Ibid.
19. Ibid.
20. Ibid.
21. Martin Larson, The Federal Reserve, 10.
22. Robinson, Proofs of Conspiracy, 57-156.
23. Ibid, 58-60.
24. Ibid.
25. Ibid, 58.
26. Ibid.
27. Epperson, R.E., The New World Order (Tucson: Publius
Press, 1990), 110.
28. Ibid, 84
29. Karl Marx and Frederick Engels, The Communist Manifesto (NY: International Publishers, 1948), Point #5, 30.

30. Chaitken, Treason in America, 53.
31. Ibid, 5-19.
32. Ibid.
33. Ibid.
34. Ibid.
35. Ibid.
36. James D. Horan, Confederate Agent, A Discovery in History, 16.
37. William McIlhany II, Klandestine, 12.
38. Epperson, Unseen Hand, 155.
39. Abraham Lincoln, Speech in Springfield, IL, January 1837.
40. Epperson, Unseen Hand, 160. The Knights of the Golden Circle was the fountainhead of the assination.

Chapter 20: History of the False Prophet
Post Civil War

1. G.G. McGreer, The Conquest of Poverty, 169.
2. Irwin Ungar, The Greenback Era, 1865-1869, 352-3, 356-61, 370.
3. Ibid.
4. Alexander Del Mar, History of Money in America, 36.
5. Chaitkin, Treason in America, 291-304.
6. Ibid.
7. Ibid.
8. Ibid.
9. Ungar, The Greenback Era, 352-3, 356-61, 370.
10. Ibid.
11. Norburn, Honest Money, 29-35.
12. Griffin, Fourth Reich, 88.
13. Norburn, Honest Money, 33.
14. H.S. Kenan, The Federal Reserve Bank; the Most Fantastic and Unbelievable Fraud in History (Los Angeles: The Noontide Press, 1966, rev. 1967), 48.
15. Mullins, Secrets of the Federal Reserve, 16.
16. Robinson, Proofs of Conspiracy. George Washington made this famous statement in response to the notion of a central bank controlled by an elite group of men.
17. Constitution of the United States of America. POWERS OF CONGRESS: Article 1, Section 8, Paragraph 5.

Chapter 21: History of the False Prophet
Anglo-America

1. Clarence Kelly, Conspiracy Against God and Man
(Belmont, MA: Western Islands, 1974). The whole book is a
historical record of the conspiracy.
2. Skousen, The Naked Capitalist, 27-29.
3. Carroll Quigley, Tragedy and Hope; A History of the
World in Our Times, 270-268.
4. Ibid, 130.
5. Ibid.
6. Carroll Quigley, Anglo-American Establishment (Books in
Focus, 1981), 33-34.
7. Skousen, The Naked Capitalist, 31.
8. Ibid.
9. The World Crisis: The Aftermath, 147.
10. Quigley, Tragedy and Hope, 132-133.
11. Ibid, 951.
12. Lawrence Shoup & William Minter, The Imperial Brain
Trust (NY: Monthly Review Press, 1977), 1-56.
13. Phoebe Courtney, The C.F.R., 36.
14. Lkousen, The Naked Capitalist, 31.
15. Ibid.
16. Ibid.
17. The Review of the News, April 9, 1980, 37-38.
18. Skousen, The Naked Capitalist, 54.
19. Ibid.
20. Ibid, 54.

Chapter 22: The Two Horned Beast

1. Quigley, The Anglo-American Establishment, 3-14.
2. Sheldon Emry, Billions for Bankers, Debts for the People:
How Did it Happen? (Phoenix: America's Promise Radio,
1967).
3. Ibid.
4. Chaitking, Treason in America, 293-295.
5. Griffin, Descent into Slavery, 66.

6. Ibid.
7. Kelly, Conspiracy, 173.

Chapter 25: The Image of the Beast

1. Vines, Expository Dictionary,, 2:243-4.
2. Ibid, 4:325-6.
3. Ibid, 2:337 & 1: 149.
4. George Gurben, Annenburg School of Communication.
5. Ibid.
6. TV, The Media, 72-73.
7. Ibid.
8. Ibid.

Chapter 29: Laser Scanning Systems

1. Roger Palmer, The Bar Code Book (Heleners Publ. Co., 1989), 11-14. Also, for complete history on bar code, consult, Reading Between the Lines, by Craig Harmon and Russ Adams (Heleners Publ. Co., 1984).
2. Ibid, 19.
3. Ibid.
4. Ibid.
5. Ibid, 22.
6. Mary Stewart Relfe, The New Money System (Montgomery, AL: Ministry Inc., 1981), 54.
7. Ibid, 47-53.

Bibliography

1. Barnes, H.F. Pearl Harbor A Quarter Century Later, Clackamas, OR: Emissary Publications, 1968.
2. Boer, H.R. A Short History of the Church, Grand Rapids: Eerdmans, 1976.
3. Carr, J.J. The Twisted Cross, Shreveport, Huntington House, 1985.
4. Chaitkin, A. Treason in America, NY: New Benjamin Franklin House, 1985.
5. Commanger, H.S.Documents of American History, NY: Appleton, 1949.
6. Courtney, Phoebe, The C.F.R.
7. Del Mar, Alexander History of Money in America
8. DeMoss, A. The Rebirth of America, U.S.A.: DeMoss, 1986.
9. Douglas, J.D. Red Cocaine, Atlanta: Clarion House, 1990.
10. Epperson, R.E. The New World Order, Tucson: Publius Press, 1990.
11. Epperson, R.E. The Unseen Hand, Tucson: Publius Press, 1985.
12. Fry, L. Waters Flowing Eastward, New Orleans: Flanders Hall, 1988.
13. Griffin, D. Fourth Reich of the Rich, Clackamas, OR: Emissary Publications, 1976.
14. Griffin, D. Descent Into Slavery, Clackamas, OR: Emissary Publications, 1978.
15. Heiden, C. Der Fuehrer, Boston: Houghton Mifflin, 1944.
16. Hislop, A. The Two Babylons, Neptune, NJ: Loizeaux Brothers, 1916.
17. Horan, James D. Confederate Agent; A Discovery in History.
18. Hunt, D. Peace, Prosperity and the Coming Holocaust, Eugene, OR: Harvest House, 1983.
19. Kelly, C. Conspiracy Against God and Man, Belmont, MA: Western Islands, 1974.
20. Kenan, H.S. The Federal Reserve Bank; the Most Fantastic and Unbelievable Fraud in History, Los Angeles: The Noontide Press, 1966 (rev. 1967).

21. Larson, Martin The Federal Reserve
22. Lindsey, Hal The Late Great Planet Earth, Grand Rapids: Zondervan, 1970.
23. McGreer, G.G. The Conquest of Poverty.
24. McIlhany, William II Klandestine.
25. Marrs, T. Millennium Austin, TX: Living Truth Publishers, 1990.
26. Marshall, Peter The Light and the Glory, Old Tappan, NJ: Fleming H. Revell, 1977.
27. Marx, Karl and Frederick Engels The Communist Manifesto, NY: International Publishers, 1948.
28. Mullins, Eustace The Secrets of the Federal Reserve, Stauton, VA: Bankers Research Institute, 1985.
29. Myers, Philip Ancient History.
30. New American Standard Bible, Open Bible Edition, Camden, NJ: Nelson, 1979.
31. Norburn, C.S. Honest Money, Ashville, NC: New Puritan Library, 1983.
32. Norburn, C.S. Honest Government, Ashville, NC: New Puritan Library, 1984.
33. Palmer, Roger The Bar Code Book, Helmers Pub, 1989.
34. Pike, W.P. Israel: Our Duty, Our Dilemma, Clackamas, OR: Emissary Publications, 1984.
35. Quigley, Carroll The Anglo-American Establishment, Books in Focus, 1981.
36. Quigley, Carroll Tragedy and Hope: A History of the World in Our Times.
37. Reeves, John The Rothschilds: Financial Rulers of the Nations.
38. Relfe, Mary Stewart The New Money System.
39. Robertson, Pat The New World Order, Word, 1991.
40. Robinson, J. Proofs of a Conspiracy, Boston: Western Islands.
41. Roebuck, Carl The World of Ancient Times, 1966.
42. Shoup, Lawrence and William Minter, The Imperial Brain Trust, NY: Monthly Review Press, 1977.
43. Skousen, C. The Naked Capitalist, Salt Lake City: 1970.
44. Star, R. History of the Ancient World, NY: Oxford Press, 1974.
45. Stewart, M. New Money or None.

46. Stormer, J. None Dare Call it Treason, Florissant, Missouri Liberty Bell Press, 1964.
47. Sutton, A.S. Wall Street and the Rise of Hitler, Seal Beach, CA. 76 Press, 1976.
48. Ungar, Irwin The Greenback Era, 1865-1869.
49. Walvord, J. The Rapture Question, Grand Rapids: Zondervan, 1976.
50. Walvord, J. Daniel - The Key to Prophetic Revelation, Chicago: Moody Press, 1971.
51. Walvord, J. The Revelation fo Jesus Christ, Chicago: Moody Press, 1966.
52. Webster, N. Surrender of an Empire, London, Emissary Publications, 1931.
53. Webster, N. The French Revolution, N. Webster, 1919.
54. Woodrow, R. Babylon Mystery Religion, 1966.

Index

1 John 2:15   33
1 Thessalonians 4:16, 17   38
1 Thessalonians 5:4   111
1 Timothy 4:1   39
1 Timothy 6:12   33
2 Corinthians 4:17, 18   198
2 Peter 3:4   161
2 Samuel 13:1-14   191
2 Samuel 13:24-39   192
2 Samuel 15:1-12   192
2 Thessalonians 2   39
2 Thessalonians 2:1-12 171, 190
2 Thessalonians 2:1-3   38
2 Thessalonians 2:2-3   41
2 Thessalonians 2:3   38
Abel   19-22, 24, 27, 28, 107
Abelism   24
Absolom   191
Agent of Antichrist   155
Ala-mahozine
    god of fortification   59
Aldrich Plan   130
Alexander the Great   68
Amnon   191
Animal sacrificial system   167
Antichrist   104
    master of Mammon   170
Antichrist, advent of   148
apostacia   38
Archangels   31
Archduke of Austria   87
Aristotle   68
Asia
    Cybele and Deous   59
Assyria   54
    and Greece   63

and Nimrod   57, 62, 63
    and Rome   63
Astarte   66
Astrology   47
Babylon   48, 60
    and Nimrod   57
Babylon (Nebuchadnezzar)   54
Babylon Mother of Harlots   66
Babylonian   29
Babylonians
    worship   58
Bacchus   68
    and Christ   69
    and Cush   69
    and Osiris   68
Bank of England   82
Bank of the United States   121
Baruch, Bernard
    and the C.F.R.   137
Battle of Waterloo   75
Bel   66
Belmont/Rothschild   126
BENELUX   100
Bickley, George L.
    and American Civil
        War   122
Bilderberger   11
Blitzkrieg warfare   153
Boleyn, Anne   80
Bolsheviks, the   89
Booth, John Wilkes
    and Internationalists   123
British Empire   74, 76, 96
    and Roman Empire   75
    The seventh head   75
Bundy, Ted   163

Bundy, Ted, serial killer
 and pornography 162
Burr, Aaron 119
 and Benedict Arnold 120
 and Henry Dundus 77
 and American Civil War 120
 and the Central Bank 131
 and Chase Manhattan Bank 120
 and the Internationalists 120
 and the Masonic Orders 120
 and the Rothschilds 120
Bush, President George
 State of Union Message 154, 172
C.F.R., the 11, 119
Caesar 18
Cain 19-24, 27, 28, 85
Cainism 23, 24, 53
Carlyle, Thomas 127
Cashless economy 172
Catherine of Aragon 80
Central Bank
 the Bank of England 83
China 76
 worship 59
Christ 22, 24, 33, 39
 Second coming 99, 189
  signs 100
Churchill, Winston 135
City of London 76, 83
 and the Rothschilds 76
 One World Government
  seat of 76
Clinton, Bill 12
 and the Bilderbergers 11
Cold war 141, 154, 172
Common Market 17, 42.
Communication system 155
Communism
 and Illuminism 142
Communist Manifesto 142
Control of colonial moneys, taxes
 and American Revolution 116
Cornwallis, General
 and India 78

Council of Foreign Relations,
 (C.F.R.)
 Anerican Round Table 136
Counterfeit currency 173
Credit card fraud 174
Crime 176
Cybel
 goddess of fortification 59
Cyrus 67, 68
Dallas Theol. Seminary 16
Daniel 16, 17, 65
 Medo-Persian Empire 67
 visions 65, 72, 103
Daniel 11:38 59, 170, 195
Daniel 11:43 170
Daniel 2:31-42 65
Daniel 2:34, 35 53
Daniel 2:35 37, 51
Daniel 2:53
Daniel 7:1-12 29
Daniel 7:19, 20, 24 52
Daniel 7:3-7 65
Daniel 7:7 72, 100, 104
Daniel 7:8 104
Daniel 8 52
Daniel 8:20 106
Daniel 9:24-26 147
Daniel 9:24-27 145
Daniel 9:26 42
Daniel 9:27 148
Darius the Great 67
Darwin, Charles 79, 127
Das Capital 142
Day of Christ 38, 41
Day of the Lord 38-39,
 41-42, 100
Desert Storm 154
Deuteronomy 15:6 117
Dionysus 68
Drugs 173
Dulles, Allen 137
Dulles, John Foster 137
Dundus, Henry
 and conquest of China 77

Eastern Establishment   12
Eastern Indian religious beliefs
   tool for world domination   78
Egypt   54, 57
   and Nimrod   57, 58
   free masonry   60
   Isis and Osiris   57, 59, 62
   religious history   61
eikon   157
Electronic Funds Transfer   186
Elizabeth I, Queen
   and East India Company   76
Emperor worship   72
Engels, Frederick   88
   and free trade   128
   and East India House   127
   British industrialist   125
   founder of Communism   127
Engles, Frederick   142
Ephesians 2:2   193
Ephesians 6:11, 12; 14-18   201
Esarharden   63
European Common Market
   16, 100, 156
Exodus 12: 21-23   107
Exodus 20:3-5a   157
exousia   108
Ezekiel   42
Ezekiel 28   31, 35, 42
Ezekiel 28:11-19   36
Ezekiel 28:13-19   32
False Prophet
   and New World Order   150
   the Second Beast   98
Federal budget deficit   172
Federal Debt   176
Federal Reserve
   Act   97, 129, 130
   and WWI   97
   and WWII   97
Federal Reserve System
   and New World Order   87
Feudalism   113
Fire storms   153

First amendment
   purpose of   80
First Beast, authority of   108
Fortification   58
Founding Fathers and
   American Constitution   80
Franklin, Benjamin   115
Free Masonry   60
   fortress Earth   60
Free masonry
   Egypt
      Isis and Osiris   60
French Revolution   81
Gallatin, Albert   121
Genesis 1   31
Genesis 10:8, 9   46
Genesis 11:1-9   46
Genesis 12:3   107
Genesis 2:17   20
Genesis 22:8   107
Genesis 3:15   46
Genesis 4:15   27
Genesis 4:3, 4   20
Genesis 4:4   107
Genesis 4:5-7   22
Gentile world-rule   49
Georgetown University   12
Global Empire   17, 153
Global kingdom   37
Global religious order   46
Global socialism   149
Global socialistic state   142
Global system
   counterfeit mil. kingdom   190
Global World Empire
   15-17, 52, 81, 98
   eighth head of the Beast   96
Global World Government
   16, 28, 48, 131, 139, 155
Global World Order   18, 53
Globalism   85
God of fortresses   170
Golden Club   126
Graduated income tax   132

Granville, Prime Minister   115
Great Britain   139
Greece   54
    Ceres   59
    Irene and Plutus   59
Guided missile technology   154
Gurban, George   159
Habakkuk 3:16-19   202
Hamilton, Alexander   119
    and Aaron Burr   120
Harvard   12
Health care   176
Hebrews 10:24-25   38
Hebrews 11:4   24
Hebrews 13:5   198
Hebrews 9:22   24
Henry VIII, King   80
Herter, Christian   137
Hiroshima   153
Hitler, Adolf   16, 18, 37,
    89, 153
    and antisemitism   93
Holiness of God   167
House, Col. Edward   88, 137
    and Internationalists   89
Illegal immigration   174
Image of the Beast   156
immorality   162
India   58, 76
    and Brirish opium trade   78
    and East India Company   77
    Isi and Iswara   58
Industrial Revolution   142
International Bankers
    War revenues   97
International Bankers, the
    and WWI & WWII   87
International free trade   142
International Globalism   128
Internationalists   11, 76,
    126, 140, 150
    and peace   86
    and French Revolution   81
    and war   86

Iran   67
Isaiah 11:11, 12   144
Isaiah 11:6-8   144
Isaiah 14   31, 35, 42
Isaiah 14:12   97
Isaiah 14:12-14   35, 195
Isaiah 14:13   190
Isaiah 43:14   67
Isaiah 45:1   67
Ishtar
    and Easter   66
Israel
    State of   52
Jackson, Andrew   121
Japan
    worship   59
Jefferson, Thomas   120
    and Central Bank   121, 131
Jekyll Island   16, 17, 129, 137
Jeremiah 22:30   194
Jeremiah 51:25   51
Jerusalem   52
Jesus   22, 24, 33
    brith celebration   47
    perfect sacrifice   167
    second coming   52
        signs   41
Jews return to Israel   145
John   53
    visions   75, 104
John 12:23 KJV   19
John 14:27   198
John 16:33   202
John 3:16   199
Judas   195
Judeo-Christian ethic   164
Judeo-Christian values   78
Kahn, Otto
    and the C.F.R.   137
Kakos   7
Kennedy, John F.
    and the Internationalists   123
Kissinger, Henry   11
Knights of Golden Circle   122

Lamb
  as a type of Christ   107
Late Great Planet Earth   16
Law   21, 22, 65, 165
  and Kaballah   67
  and oral tradition   66
  and Talmud   66
  as a covenant   166
Leviticus   66
Leviticus 17:11b   167
Leviticus 20:17   192
Lincoln, Abraham   121, 126
  and the Central Bank   131
Lincoln greenbacks   122, 128
Lindbergh, Charles   153
Lindsay, Hal   16
Lippmann, Walter   137
List, Frederick
  and German Republic   127
Lucifer   31, 32, 36, 37
  mutiny   42
Luftwaffe   153
Luke 16:9   171
Luke 21:24   52
Luke 21:28   42, 198
Luke 21:34, 35   145, 149
Malthus, Thomas   127
Mammon   81
Mark of Cain   27, 28
Mark of Beast   17, 27, 28, 29
Marx, Karl   88, 93, 141
  disciple of Engles   127
Masonic Order
  and the Illuminati   118
Masonic secret societies   117
  and the Rothschilds   117
Matthew 1:24   194
Matthew 24   39
Matthew 24:6   38, 140
Matthew 6:10   33
Matthew 6:24   170
Medo-Persia   54
Medo-Persian empire   29
Military equilibrium   141

Mill, John Stuart   127
  and East India Company   79
Millennial Kingdom   144, 149
Millennial kingdom   190
Millennial reign   145, 189
Millennium   12
Millennium of Messiah   149
Milner, Alfred   133
Mind control network   155
Molock   157
Monroe Doctrine   142
Morality   162
Morgan, J. P.
  and the C.F.R.   137
Mosaic Law   21, 66
Moses   21
Mystery Babylon   50, 53
Mystery Babylon
  Mother of Harlots   45, 51, 70
    global religious order   46
Mystery Babylon the City   46, 47
Mystery of Iniquity   20
Mystery of Righteousness   20
Mystery religion
  free masonry   60
Mystery religions
  Nimrod   47
Nagasaki   153
Napalm bombs   153
Napoleon   75
Nazi Party   16, 93
Neo-feudalism   132
New Age
  and Indian Hinduism   78
New Age movement
  and East India House   79
New cashless econ. sys.   173
New Covenant, the   167
New economic system   171
New World Econ. Sys.   183, 188
New World Order   17, 23-24, 33
  60, 74, 86, 87, 98, 110, 133,
  139, 142, 150, 158, 188
New World Order Econ.   176

New York   15, 89, 143
Nimrod   18, 46, 47, 57,
    58, 60, 69
  and Antichrist   46
  and Christmas tree   47
  and Kaballah   67
  Babylonian kingdom   47, 51,
    57, 66
    and Egypt   61
    Medo-Persian Empire   68
    and Assyrian Empire   63
  centaur   58
  deified   46, 58
    and Bacchus   68
    Ninus   60, 62
  fortifications   47
Nimrod, father of
  Cush   46, 69
Nimrod, wife of
  Semiramus   57
    Cybel/Rhea   60
    worship   59, 60
Nuclear weapons   86, 153
One World Culture   159
One World Empire   17
One World worship   158
One World Government   18,
    37, 43, 101, 103, 126, 164
One World Order   33, 123
One World System   108
Order of Illuminati   88, 118
  and Communism   119
Pagan Indian religions
  British state run religions   78
Paterson, William
  and the Bank of England   115
Pax Romana   72
Peace movement   149
Petty, William, Prime Minister
  American independence   77
PIN number   185
Plato   68, 134
Pneuma   158
Poneros   7

Pornography   162, 163
Princeton   12
Proofs of A Conspiracy   118
prophecy   12
Prophets
  Daniel   18, 28-29, 42, 51, 53
  Ezekiel   32
  Jeremiah   18
  John   13, 17, 29, 53, 54
  Jonah   18
Protestant Reformation   76, 80
Protocols of Illuminati   92, 117
Protocols of Learned Elders of
  Zion   90
Proverbs 22:7   88
Proverbs 23:1, 2   170
Proverbs 23:5   169
Psalm 30:7   50
Psalm 69:22   145
Psalm 74   8
Quigley, Dr. Carroll   12, 136
Rapture   38
Republicanism vs
  Feudalism/Communism   128
Revelation 12   42
Revelation 12:4   32
Revelation 13   12, 28, 29
Revelation 13:1   73, 104
Revelation 13:1-11   29
Revelation 13:11   106, 140
Revelation 13:12   108, 109, 139
Revelation 13:13   151, 154
Revelation 13:13-18   29
Revelation 13:14, 15   156
Revelation 13:16, 17   171
Revelation 13:16-18   183
Revelation 13:17   169
Revelation 13:18   179
Revelation 13:3   53, 85, 95,
  105, 149
Revelation 13:4   90, 132
Revelation 17:1-5   64
Revelation 17:10   54, 70, 75
Revelation 17:10, 11   53
Revelation 17:11   95, 96, 156

Revelation 17:3, 4   69
Revelation 17:5   57
Revelation 17:7-13   50
Revelation 17:9-11   98
Revelation 18:1   45
Revelation 2:27   190
Revelation 7:10   72
Rhea
   Cybel   60
   Semiramus   60
Rhodes, Cecil   119, 133
Rockefeller, David   11
Rockefeller, John D.
   and the C.F.R.   137
Roman Empire   17, 42,
   54, 75
   and Common Market   100
Rome
   Jupiter   59
   Mary and Jesus   59
Rothschild, Nathan
   and Internationalists   82
Rothschilds, the
   and the Free-masons   117
   and the State of Israel   92
Round Table, the   119, 136
Ruskin, John   119, 133
Russia   89
Satan   17-18, 24, 32-33,
   36-37, 43
   Global kingdom   47
   Mystery Babylon   45
   world religions   43, 45, 46
Schift, Jacob
   and the C.F.R.   137
SCUD missiles   154
Second Beast
   Agent of Antichrist   101
   lamb-like appearance   107
   Wolf in sheep's clothing   107
Shalmaneser   63
Solzhenitsyn   78
Star Wars technology   154
State of Israel   144, 145

Strategic Defense Initiative   154
Supremacy Act   80
Tamar   191
Televangelists   8
Ten-member confederacy   51
The Condition of Working Class
   128
Thoreau, Henry David   79
Throne of David   189
Tibet
   worship   59
Tiglath-pileser   63
Titus   42
Tragedy and Hope   12
Tree of life   20, 21
Tree of knowledge of good and
   evil 20, 21
Tri-lateral Commission   11
United Nations   154
Universal computer access
   number   186
Universal product code   179
Untaxed underground econ.   174
UPC symbol
   machine readable code   181
Victoria, Queen
   and the East India Company   79
Vietnam   153
Wall Street
   and the Third Reich   91
Warburg, Max   89
Warburg, Paul
   and the C.F.R.   137
   and Internationalists   97, 130
   architect of Federal Reserve   89
Ward, Rear Admiral Chester
   and the C.F.R.   138
Washington, George   142
   and Aaron Burr   120
   and the Central Bank   130, 131
   and the Illuminati   118
Weishaupt, Adam   18, 88, 117,
   142

Wilson, Woodrow
   and the Federal Reserve Act   97
   and the League of Nations   88
   and WWI   88
World ecological movement   149
Wright Brothers   151
Zodiac
   and Nimrod   47
Zoe   158

ACKNOWLEDGEMENTS

There have been so many people who prayed for me during the course of the writing of this book. To all those great friends I give a heartfelt thanks.

In the initial stages Ed and Kelly King were a tremendous encouragement by their continued help in typing and editing the notes accumulated over the past six years.

I also would like to acknowledge Anne Brown, who spent many hours in the final edit of the manuscript and worked so hard to finish the typesetting in a timely fashion.

Thanks to Fred Renich who did all the fine tuning and engineering of the last stages of production.

Most of all I must acknowledge the spiritual support of my wife Jan, who endured all the hard times and continued to believe, praying me through to completion.

And thanks to the Lord, who would not let me give up.

ABOUT THE AUTHOR

Ken Klein has been a follower of the Lord Jesus Christ for twenty-three years. Coming from a Jewish background he had virtually no Christian education or training until he was saved in 1969 at the age of twenty-four.

While attending the University of Oregon on a football scholarship he studied Religion, Psychology and Sociology in the Liberal Arts department. His college athletic career flourished and he elected to play professional football with both the San Francisco Forty-niners and the Houston Oilers. In the off season he returned to school and received his Bachelor of Science degree.

His professional sports career ended through a series of injuries, and like many athletes, Ken fell into trouble with drugs. During this time of depression he found the Lord. Immediately upon his conversion he developed a voracious appetite for the Scriptures.

After several years of study he became college pastor for a large church in Eugene, Oregon. The college work grew. Many young people were saved and went into the ministry. Ken's ministry developed into church planting where he pioneered and pastored three churches in Oregon, Washington, and California.

In 1984 Ken authored his first book, called *A Strong Delusion*, which was a chronicle of his involvement in drugs and the New Age Movement. He has been on national television many times as a guest on Pat Robertson's 700 club and on many occasions with Paul Crouch's Trinity Broadcasting.

His interest in both the New Age Movement and drugs, which stemmed from his own involvement, led him into a deep study of the prophetic writings. During the last seven years he has worked on the manuscript for this new work, *The False Prophet*.

GET OUR NEWSLETTER
COMPLIMENTARY COPY — "STORM WARNING"

You can receive a complimentary copy of "Storm Warning," Ken Klein's bi-monthly newsletter. "Storm Warning" deals with current events which are breaking around the world, and that line up with Biblical prophecy. You will want to keep track of the ongoing rush to the New World Order. If you want to subscribe now the annual subscription is $18, but we will send a complimentary copy if you will write:

Ken Klein Ministries
P.O. Box 40922
Eugene, OR 97404

PROPHECY CONFERENCE ALBUM

You will want to hear Ken Klein's three hour Prophecy Conference on the New Age Movement and the New World Order. In a beautifully packaged album with three one-hour audio cassettes you can listen and study these amazing prophecies coming to pass in our time.

The prophecy package comes with or without the book *The False Prophet*.
1. **Three hour Prophecy Conference Album**
   three audio tapes with book *The False Prophet* $30 plus $3 postage.
2. **Three hour Prophecy Conference Album**
   three audio tapes (no book included) $18 plus $2 postage

THE FALSE PROPHET IN AUDIO

Good News for those who don't like to read!

The False Prophet is also in an audio book form. You can obtain a copy for yourself or friend by sending $16 plus $2 postage and handling to Ken Klein Ministries (see above for address or phone number).

KEN KLEIN PROPHECY CONFERENCES

Would you like to bring this message to your community?

Ken Klein Prophecy Conferences on the New World Order are being heard around the country in and outside churches. If you would like to bring this powerful and life-changing conference to your city or church please write to the Ken Klein Ministries at the address noted above.